Learning to Learn

The Waldon Approach has been integral to our work in facilitating the development of learning foundations for our pupils. It provides the pupils with the basis for cognitive development and it complements our relationship-based approach perfectly, helping us to ensure that pupils' learning develops hand in hand with their emotional development. This book is an invaluable resource for any specialist setting.

CATHERINE BERNIE, DEPUTY HEAD

I have used 'Learning to Learn' as an essential pedagogical approach to teach those early learning skills. I have found it really effective, especially for my students with severe autism. The book is full of great ideas which can be applied directly into our daily teaching.

**PETER MASARYK, ASSOCIATE PRINCIPAL,
ROSEHILL SCHOOL, NEW ZEALAND**

Learning to Learn

How to teach children with learning difficulties or autism to learn

by Merete Hawkins

A STEP BY STEP GUIDE
to the Waldon Approach – Learning by doing

Structured activities to develop
the core cognitive capacities

www.peculiaritypress.com

ISBN 978-1-912384-08-2

This work first published 2019
by Peculiarity Press, an imprint of Leigh & Glennie Ltd.
The Business Centre, Greys Green Farm, Henley-on-Thames RG 9 4QG, UK.
© Leigh & Glennie Ltd 2019.

The text of this work © Merete Hawkins 2019.

Merete Hawkins has asserted her right under the Copyright Designs and Patents Act, 1998, to be identified as the author of this work.

All rights reserved. Without limiting the rights under copyright reserved above, no part of this publication may be reproduced, stored or introduced into a retrieval system, or transmitted, in any form or by any means (electronic, mechanical, photocopying, recording, or otherwise), without the prior written permission of the author and publisher of this book.

The author and publisher are not responsible for your use of the information contained in these pages, in any way whatsoever. The author and publisher do not assume and hereby disclaim any liability to any party for any loss, damage, or disruption caused by errors or omissions, whether they result from negligence, accident, or any other cause.

The author, in her capacity as a teacher, does not hold herself out to be a medical or health professional, and in case of questions or concerns, specialist medical knowledge should be sought by the reader. Every child develops at his own individual pace and the author cannot and does not guarantee a particular result from using this book. The author and publisher advise readers to take full responsibility for ensuring the appropriate use and safety of materials, equipment, and environment at all times.

Merete Hawkins and Peculiarity Press do not accept any responsibility for any third-party author or website referred to in this book.

Design by Jane Glennie.

CONTENTS

Foreword. By Richard Brooks — vii

Chapter 1. Introduction — 1
- The learning to learn approach — 1
- My background — 2
- How to use the book — 3
- For parents — 3
- Dedications and thank you — 4

SECTION 1. BACKGROUND AND THEORY

Chapter 2. Learning to Learn — 7
- How do children learn? — 7
- The principles of the learning to learn approach — 9
- The structured learning to learn session — 10
- Understanding Understanding – Geoffrey Waldon's theories of learning — 10

Chapter 3. Early cognitive development — 13
- Early cognitive developmental levels and milestones — 13
- Level 1. Developments in the first year: Fundamental movement abilities — 15
- Level 2. Developments in the second year: Continuant capacity — 17
- Level 3. Developments in the third year: Learning to learn capacities — 19
- Growth of the learning capacities — 20
- The importance of hand-held tools — 21

Chapter 4. Learning difficulties and their impact on learning — 23
- Learning difficulties and the impact on the ability to learn — 23
- Autism and learning — 24
- Language, communication and interaction — 25
- Emotion and learning — 25
- Challenging behaviours — 26

SECTION 2. IMPLEMENTATION

Chapter 5. The practical implementation of the learning to learn approach — 31
- The key principles of the learning to learn session — 31
    - *General advice on using the approach*
    - *How to keep the child engaged*
- Getting started — 33
    - *Equipment*
    - *Organising the classroom and the work areas*
    - *How to give hand-over-hand support*
    - *Touch-sensitive children*

▶ The structured session 38
    Planning the content
    Balance of the lesson content
    Length of the sessions
    How to extend familiar activities with variations
    Generalisation of the learning to learn abilities

▶ Further advice 41
    Managing challenging behaviours during the session
    Social interaction during the session
    The reasons for not giving praise
    Important note: Look after yourself

Chapter 6. Initial assessment of the learning to learn abilities 43
  ▶ How to carry out an assessment 44
  ▶ Initial assessment framework 49

SECTION 3. PRACTICAL ACTIVITIES

  ▶ Introduction 52

Chapter 7. Level 1 Fundamental movement abilities and activities 53
  ▶ Movement and physical effort 54
  ▶ Range and use of space 55
  ▶ Picking up and putting in 58
  ▶ Complementary use of hands and tool use 61

Chapter 8. Level 2 Continuant capacity and activities 67
  ▶ Continuant capacity activities 69

Chapter 9. Level 3 Learning to learn capacities and activities 76
  ▶ The development of the learning to learn capacities 76
  ▶ Matching 79
  ▶ Sorting 91
  ▶ Seriation 105
  ▶ Drawing 120
  ▶ Brick-building 129
  ▶ Coding 138

APPENDICES

  ▶ 1: Learning to learn equipment 145
  ▶ 2: Learning to learn lesson plan 148
  ▶ 3: Developmental framework of the learning to learn capacities 150
  ▶ 4: Extracts from lesson feedback 155
  ▶ 5: FAQ 159
  ▶ 6: Further information and contact 161

FOREWORD

by Richard Brooks

Discovering the work of Geoffrey Waldon was the most important moment of my professional life. It opened up a new way to understand learning and every aspect of development, and it gave me a wide-open potential for designing learning activities tailored to the ability of each particular child. Introducing the ideas to other professionals, it was encouraging to find some who quickly saw their importance. Many of these were teachers for whom I already had a great respect. Merete was one of these. She was well known as a teacher of energy and creativity, who was always systematically looking to improve her practice, researching and experimenting to get the best results. Her interest in Waldon's ideas came quite early in her career, and since then she has continued to study other approaches in depth. It pleases me enormously that it is the Waldon Approach that has remained the main strand of her thinking and has inspired this tremendous book.

Geoffrey himself never completed a book, though he wrote a great deal. One reason his work was unfinished is implicit in his working practice. Re-thinking child development, he was always questioning his own ideas and refining them further. He could never feel he had come to a final right answer, because, as he wrote, he would uncover new fundamental issues. He saw this same process in the learning of children. The development of a child's understanding does not aim towards end points and the mastery of particular skills. It is a process where new experience is constantly created as the child does more of what she can already do across the full range of her abilities, with variations being accidental and inevitable. Merete often emphasises this when she is describing how a lesson should flow – the need to leave activities unfinished with the teacher unconcerned about completion, aware that the learning happens during the process. And if that process takes a tortuous, winding, unfinished path, the learning may well be the stronger. I'm pleased she didn't take this too fully to heart in her own case and did manage to finish a book which will be a valuable guide to teachers and parents.

Waldon was a neurologist, who worked every day as a teacher (or 'facilitator') with disabled children, simultaneously developing their understanding and his own. Each lesson was a research opportunity that took his ideas forward. Parents and teachers watched him, fascinated by the unique atmosphere of the 'asocial' lesson, and the wide range of practical activities designed to reproduce the learning of ordinary children. The materials are chosen for their simplicity, so that the facilitator can focus with the greatest possible clarity on the child's movements, because it is through his movements that he shows his understanding. Merete is also a teacher who seems to generate new ideas and variations effortlessly in her work. Taking Waldon's ideas and activities as her starting point she has shown how they can be varied and enriched. She also shows, in these pages, how clearly she is able to explain the purpose of the activities, the preparation of materials, the pitfalls to avoid and the ways to shape them to the needs of widely differing children. She has organised the chapters in a way that makes it easy to follow as a guide and, at every stage, she has explained the what, how and why of each activity so that the careful reader can feel confident about getting started and building her own understanding.

Over the years, the greatest gift I have had from Waldon has been many hours of mesmerising observation. There have been so many wonderful moments when I have been able to stand silently beside a child, almost holding my breath, watching them make hundreds of small decisions, sometimes pausing and unmaking them, light-bulbs coming on, then fading and blinking on again, as they self-correct, think and rethink. This unbroken flow of concentrated activity, where the teacher is forgotten because the activity itself has absorbed the child's attention, absorbs me totally, and it also convinces me that her understanding is growing and, above all, that she is learning to trust her own judgement and learning how to learn effectively in the future.

I am so pleased that Merete's book will make it possible for more people to take up this fascinating approach to helping children and I am confident that, with such clear guidance, many will gain from it the same satisfaction it has given to me.

INTRODUCTION: LEARNING TO LEARN

A step by step guide to the Waldon Approach for children with learning difficulties or autism

All children enjoy the feelings of being engrossed in an activity and making sense of it through doing. The learning to learn approach teaches children how to learn and understand through active doing, based on the insights and practical method described by Dr Geoffrey Waldon.

Waldon observed young children at play and he noticed how they explored and used the objects in their environment; this led to the recognition that meaning comes from movement and the use of the hands. The child's fundamental movement abilities are laid down during the first year of life, and his mental capacities for organising information and understanding the world are built on this foundation; it follows a pattern of development which is universal to all children, regardless of their abilities.

The capacities to explore and learn from experience are impaired in most children with learning difficulties or autism. Their play experiences are often quite limited, or they get stuck in set behaviours because they don't know what to do. Their foundations for learning might not be solid and they have gaps in their understanding. In order to help these children progress, they need an intervention based on this universal pattern of development with an emphasis on the early stages where the foundations are laid. That is the rationale for the learning to learn approach.

- Children enjoy learning when the activities are perfectly tuned to their developmental level. They will get absorbed and play for long periods of time.
- Effortful games with variations will build the foundations; the adult helps the child to become active, fully focused and able to stay engaged in the learning activities.
- The teaching approach is active and non-verbal; the adult guides the child's hands to participate in the activities and shows him what to do. This mirrors how young children play when they are by themselves: they explore objects and what they can do. They learn by doing and not through talking or explanation.
- The cognitive developmental framework has clearly defined levels and stages and describes the stepping-stones to the first 60 months of life.
- The step by step guidance describes how to present the activities at all stages, supported by a wealth of ideas of how to play.
- The concept of **theme and variation** is central to the approach; the child is provided with a wide range of learning opportunities at every level, to broaden his understanding.

The focus of this book is on the child's cognitive development and it does not address his social interaction and emotional growth; these abilities are of course equally important and complement the cognitive development; however, they require quite different types of interventions and extensive guidance on relationship-based programmes can be found elsewhere. With a carefully balanced curriculum with focus on both the cognitive and social and emotional development, the whole child will grow.

My background

I came across the Waldon Approach early in my career when I was teaching in a special resource unit for children with autism. I quickly realised that this unusual approach was essential when teaching children with Special Educational Needs and it became the core of my work throughout my teaching career. This was my way forward when a child was hard to engage; it gave me the understanding of early development and a method that worked, and I experienced the children's joy in learning.

Dr Geoffrey Waldon was a neurologist who worked with young children in the 1970s and 1980s. His approach is based on his observations and practical experience of interventions with the children.

 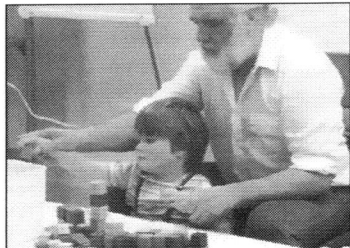 

Video stills of Geoffrey Waldon working with children

During his lifetime, Waldon disseminated his work through workshops with professionals in the field as well as parents; he had a strong following in Oxfordshire where I worked in the Autism Service and the SEN schools. Waldon sadly died before he wrote a book, but he thankfully left an extensive collection of papers which outline his profound insights.

I decided to write this book to translate Waldon's approach into practice. I have devised a developmental framework and a step by step approach with practical activities which gives parents and professionals tools to engage children and foster their cognitive development.

In my work I refer to the approach as the **learning to learn approach** instead of the Waldon Approach. The reason is that I have introduced some changes to Waldon's original approach, reflecting my own experiences of what worked well for me with the many children I have taught. Over the years I have seen the benefit of flexibility and of adapting the method to suit the special needs of every child. Geoffrey Waldon's approach is unique and the knowledge base and method must not be lost. I hope this book will inspire teachers, parents and others to learn, apply and develop this technique. The children deserve it.

How to use the book

This book is intended for school staff as well as parents working with children with learning difficulties and/or autism. The book describes how children learn and the critical stages in their development to become active learners, followed by a resource of games and activities to promote their growing understanding. The book is designed to provide the theoretical background first, leading on to the step by step programme of interventions.

I have developed the learning to learn framework, which describes three significant developmental levels, as I see it; it is based on Waldon's descriptors for the first 60 months of development. This framework gives a structure which helps us to identify a child's current level of understanding and following on from that, enables us to plan activities which will engage him and facilitates his progress.

Section 1 provides a summary of some of Waldon's insights into how children learn through doing; this is essential background knowledge as it helps us to fully understand the approach in practice. It will give an appreciation of why the structured learning to learn session is so important to build the learning foundations. The three critical levels of early development are clearly explained and this demonstrates how every new ability is born out of competence at the previous level. The impact of having a learning difficulty is also considered as is the way forward.

Section 2 describes the practical implementation of the approach: how to work with the child, translating the principles into practice. The structured session is outlined in great detail aiming to provide sufficient information for everyone to get started. The second part is guidance on how to carry out an initial assessment and record the observations; this is the starting point for planning.

Finally, **section 3** is a resource of activities. It is divided into the three levels, one chapter for each. The developmental steps are explained and accompanied by an extensive source of practical ideas. The games also come with suggestions of how to introduce variations to increase the learning opportunities. This programme contains ideas for activities up to the stage where the child is fully equipped with the skills to learn, which is roughly the developmental age of about 60 months.

It is critical to remember that the purpose of the activities is to develop the child's understanding, the activities are NOT the goal in themselves. Every experience must aim to expand the child's understanding and build his skills to learn.

I always stay faithful to Waldon's original concepts but I have in places introduced a slightly different vocabulary to describe them. This decision was based on my experience of training staff who at times found some of the original terminology somewhat confusing and I believe these changes make it more accessible.

This book provides a thorough background to the Waldon approach and how to implement and incorporate the method in the classroom or at home; however, attending workshops and receiving training from others in the field, are important to become a skilled practitioner.

For parents

Parents and children generally learn together, but when a child has a learning difficulty, this may not be quite so easy. This book provides an understanding of how children learn, explanation of the abilities that underpin learning and guidance for parents to create the right sort of experiences for their child to become engrossed in and enjoy.

Children with learning difficulties may not explore widely or they get stuck in self-stimulating activities. They need more direction of how to play and what to do; the method we use must be appropriate for the child's current level of understanding. In the early years, children learn from activities, not by talking, explaining or being told what to do. They need simple toys and materials which can be used in many different ways such as empty boxes, bricks, pegs, conkers etc. They need long periods to play without being distracted by electronic toys and screens such as the television, tablets and phones. These electronic gadgets can take the children's attention away from real play and learning experiences.

The description of the learning to learn approach is mostly given with reference to the school environment. For you as parents, the principles remain the same as the programme outlines how to work with your child at his current level of understanding and gives lots of ideas for appropriate play activities. The purpose of the games is to enhance a child's general abilities; take for example putting bricks into a saucepan has the purpose of practising a range of movement patterns; sweeping bricks into a dustpan is also about becoming familiar with the movements and the space around the body. It is not learning the skills of tidying up or cleaning. More specific skills like counting or naming the colours come later and they are not part of this approach; however, the child is ready to learn these skills when his learning to learn foundations are solidly built.

The practical ideas are the starting point to develop your own activities, using the equipment you have available in your house. Lots of 'rubbish' or 'loose bits' can be used to create games, take for example an empty screw-top bottle is great for posting games, an empty chocolate box can be filled with fir cones and so on. In chapter 5 there is a section on how to extend familiar activities with variations, which gives more insights into broadening activities and keeping your child engaged.

It is worth bearing in mind that doing activities continue throughout life and they give us enjoyment as well as being a practical necessity. We use our hands to carry bags, chop vegetables, dig holes, hang up washing, organise shoes into pairs, putting shopping in the trolley at the supermarket and so on; everyday activities are a great source of meaningful occupation as well as learning. Furthermore, many people also enjoy creating with their hands, be it woodwork, making jewellery, model making or drawing. These are all extensions of the skills learnt early on.

Use this book to understand how your child learns and how to create meaningful activities; it will open the door to progress and the two of you having fun together.

Note

In order to help with fluency in reading, I made the arbitrary decision to refer to the child as 'he' and to the staff or parent as 'she'. However, I would like to invite the reader to treat the pronoun choice as a matter of speech, and please consider all references to be unisex.

Dedications

I wish to dedicate this book to two inspirational teachers I worked with in Oxfordshire, Richard Brooks and Sue Saville and to the memory of Sheila Coates, who all helped to change the lives of many children with autism for the better. Thank you.

I wish to thank Richard Brooks for introducing me to the method and his help in writing the book;

I wish to thank Sibylle Janert for her comments and regular feedback throughout the process and her encouragement to keep going; to Keith, my husband, for reading, commenting and listening to me talk about Waldon, and finally to all the children I have had the privilege to learn from.

SECTION 1: BACKGROUND AND THEORY

LEARNING TO LEARN

The learning to learn approach evolved from Geoffrey Waldon's insight, that meaning comes from movement; he observed that 'from doing we learn'. The fundamental movement abilities develop in the first year of life and continue through countless experiences to evolve and form the foundation for all higher levels of understanding. Children are ready to learn when they can engage, explore and focus their attention, thus enabling the mental processes of analysing, organising and applying their knowledge. This is the corner-stone of the learning to learn approach.

How do children learn to learn?

The human baby is born with no specialised skills or abilities, but he is primed to move and he is internally driven to interact with the world around him. During the first and second year the foundations are laid for what becomes his **experience gathering equipment**, the necessary capacities for learning.

Learning to learn requires mastery of movements

Take a look at the new-born baby. He is essentially a trunk with four independent limbs and a head, the hands are simply extensions of his arms. During the first year of life the baby progresses quickly and almost imperceptibly gains a vast number of movement skills and a fully integrated body; the baby becomes aware of where his limbs are in space and how to use his hands. He also learns to balance and sit, to crawl and by 12 to 15 months most babies begin to toddle around. By now, they have sufficient control over their movements to decide where to go, they have the ability to choose what to be interested in, what to pick up, carry around and where to go with it. They have all the movement skills they need to explore the world!

Learning to learn requires the skilled use of the hands

Once the baby has gained some awareness of the movements of his arms and body, he becomes aware of his hands and what they can do. He explores them in front of his face and in his mouth. He learns to pick up and hold objects with his hands. By the age of 12 months most babies are purposeful in the way they manipulate toys with their hands; they are learning about the different characteristics of each object and they do not get distracted by other toys around. They are quite literally beginning to grasp the meaning of what they are holding; they are ready for the next stage in their development.

Learning to learn requires memory of a sequence of movements

A toddler spends endless time moving objects from one place to another. As he is busy doing so, he begins to remember the order and the places where he leaves the toys; this signifies the beginning of planning a movement sequence: what to pick up and where to take it next. This behaviour of moving things around leads to a massive gain in his understanding of the objects, their different characteristics such as texture, weight, size etc. and what the objects can do: they roll, they fit inside the box, they

make a noise and so on; he begins to perceive the similarities and differences between them. By the end of the second year, the toddler has the cognitive abilities to notice and remember how objects have different properties and he can use this information in both familiar and unfamiliar situations; he has now developed the experience-gathering equipment with which his understanding will grow.

Learning to learn abilities grow before the understanding of language

The early learning to learn abilities develop before the child understands the language associated with them. These capacities, the mastery of movement, the use of hands and exploring and moving toys around in an ongoing fashion, all grow in the first two years of life. His understanding of the world is acquired through the acts of doing and only much later in his development, will he begin to attach meaning through language.

This is a critical point for teaching: the early understanding develops through doing and before language; therefore the teaching at the early levels must be through activities, not by using language to instruct or explain. The child cannot understand the meaning until he has the knowledge acquired through practical experiences. This insight led to this unique teaching method.

Annabel

Annabel spent a lot of her time standing still and looking out of the window. There was something in the patterns of leaves and the greenery which fascinated her; she loved to stare at computer screens in the same way. She didn't understand what people meant when she was told to join the group, nor did she know how to play with toys. Annabel didn't know how to learn with her hands and she was reluctant to touch anything unfamiliar.

With the gentle guidance of hand over hand, she learnt to pick up objects and put them into containers. She also started to hold onto and use scoops to transfer objects from one bowl to another, and before long she became interested in holding a thick crayon in her hand and used it to make marks on the paper. Annabel was no longer scared of moving her arms and holding objects. She became more purposeful and she was learning with her hands; she was no longer stuck in mindless staring.

The principles of the teaching approach

The principles of the learning to learn approach are to create an environment which is appropriate for the child's stage of development and to provide activities which build solid learning foundations; the approach recognises that understanding grows from the movement abilities which evolve very early on.

Children with a learning difficulty often need extra help to develop their abilities to learn and they often have an uneven profile of cognitive abilities with gaps in their understanding. With this approach, the learning conditions and experiences are provided to match the children's levels of development and this maximises the opportunities to move up the developmental ladder.

1. Early learning is through doing: from movement comes understanding. The child is engaged in a structured session with an adult, who teaches through active play with objects, exploring and moving these around; the games require effort and full engagement.

2. Children learn through variations; this is critical to the approach. Children do not set out to learn, they return to their familiar games; but as they play, unplanned variations occur which create new experiences from which they learn.

3. The teaching method is non-verbal. The children are taught by guiding their hands through activities, by showing and doing, and not by explaining. Children learn from playing with objects: they do, they notice, they understand. At the early levels, language is not involved in understanding the world.

4. During the structured session the adult does not praise or give verbal encouragement; the motivation comes from the intrinsic pleasure of doing.

5. The developmental framework provides a structure for assessment and planning. It outlines the levels and stages in the growth of the child's cognitive capacities and the underlying abilities at every level.

6. The activities should be enjoyable and the child should play without fear of failure or judgement of being right or wrong. He should feel the pleasure of being active and effortful and engrossed for lengthy periods of time.

SECTION 1: BACKGROUND AND THEORY

The structured learning to learn session

The non-verbal, structured session is special to this approach and it incorporates all the principles described above. The adult teaches by guiding the child's hands and together they engage in a range of effortful activities: picking up, putting in, lining up, sorting, building and much more. The adult sits behind the child and moves his hands, she does not give any verbal instructions or explanations. The aim is for the child to become independent and carry on without help.

This style of teaching can at first sight seem quite unusual, guiding the child through activities without talking; however, it matches perfectly the way children typically learn at this level. These structured activities provide opportunities to practise the fundamental movement skills, a chance to discover more about the many features of the materials and promote the ability to mentally organise this information.

During the non-verbal lesson there is a very close relationship between the child and the facilitator. The manner in which the adult supports the child can feel like a dance; she has to be finely tuned into the child's level of mastery, she has to constantly adapt and adjust the activities to ensure he feels at ease and succeeds.

Even though there is no talking during the session itself, conclude the lesson with a warm social interaction, share the joy of the joint experience.

Waldon working with a child in the 1980s

Understanding Understanding

This section describes in a little more detail Geoffrey Waldon's insights into how children learn and the implication for teaching, based primarily on two papers, *Understanding Understanding* (1980) and *Learning and the Origin of Understanding* (undated), which can be found on the Waldon Association website.

Waldon made a distinction between two strands of the developing mind, General Understanding and Particular Understanding. The latter refers to particular cultural and social understanding and this is specific to where the child grows up. This learning takes place in the company of others and it is shaped by the experiences of interacting with care-givers and other people in the social environment. On the other hand, General Understanding is concerned with cognitive development and this process is fundamental to all humans, regardless of culture or ability.

The General Understanding refers to the cognitive processes of making sense of experiences. Take, for example, a child playing with mud. He feels it in his hands and notices that the mud is runny but it dries on his hands, that a stone sinks to the bottom whereas a leaf stays on top, the stone is hard and the leaf is light and brittle. The child makes new discoveries which guides him to some general principles of organising information and using these experiences in the future. These early skills are unspecialised and common to all children at a similar level.

The human baby is born very dependent on his parents for survival and he has very few skills. But as human beings we develop general capacities which enable us to learn and deal with almost any situation, and these are our learning capacities: the movement skills that underpin exploring and the mental capacities to organise and apply our understanding of the world in new situations. There is a long period of learning to acquire these general capacities that equip us with the unique abilities to deal with both the expected and the unexpected; this is the foundation for all growth.

Waldon's observations of young children led him to conclude that cognitive development is rooted in movement and that meaning grows from action. During the first year of life the fundamental movement abilities develop which enable the child to interact purposefully with the world around him. Take a 9 to 10-month-old baby: he can pick up a toy and bang it on the floor, pass it from hand to hand and drop it into a box. In this play the action rather than the object is the key factor.

Geoffrey Waldon analysed the object-play behaviour of children during the second year of life and he called it continuant behaviour or continuant capacity, and described it as the **carrier phase for learning**. He recognised that this capacity is critical: the ability to plan and remember where to move objects in order and to organise these in different ways. It also lays the foundation for the next level, the general learning to learn capacities, which evolve and continue to grow throughout life. Waldon defined the many stages in their evolution and these are incorporated into this programme.

Waldon observed how a baby's play gradually became purposeful. A baby will sit and explore his toys, and as he is doing so, he will start to notice the effects of his actions and he will gradually become aware of the effects; in time, he will be able to make a conscious decision about what to do with a toy. This means the child starts to pick up the toy with the purpose of banging it on the table because he knows the sounds he can create; he has added a new behaviour to his understanding. Learning also happens when variations inadvertently occur, for example he might drop the toy, it rolls along; the child notices what happened and he starts to repeat the action in order to see the toy roll again. To quote Waldon:

> *'In short: doing leads on to increasing frequency of doing, and in due course to noticing doing, then attending to doing gives rise to understanding the doing, and (at last!) to wanting to do. It follows that a child cannot be or become aware of the purpose of his activity until that activity is a regular component of his total behaviour and is itself understood'*
> THE RISE OF INTEREST AND MOTIVATION (WALDON – UNPUBLISHED ARTICLE)

It follows that in order to facilitate a child's development, he needs many familiar activities with variations. In practice, this translates into a method which places the emphasis on consolidating established learning through well-known and active games played with many variations.

Waldon used the term motivation to describe the innate drive to move and to be effortful; the child experiences real pleasure from being active. This definition of motivation is very different from the common usage of the word, which usually equates motivation with an incentive; the former comes from within, whereas the latter requires an external goal and is given by another. Incentives are not used in this approach; when a child associates effort with enjoyment, he is driven to learn from within. This is internal motivation.

In his writing Geoffrey Waldon discusses the commonly held assumption that young children learn by imitation; however, he rejects this notion because the ability to imitate the behaviour of someone else requires recognition and therefore prior knowledge of the behaviour. A child builds up his fundamental understanding by experience; only when he reaches the higher levels of cognitive development can he analyse the sequences and actions of others. Teaching by imitation is inappropriate until the child has reached this advanced level of understanding.

Further reading can be found on **www.waldonassociation.org.uk** where there is a large number of papers including *Understanding Understanding*. There are also videos showing Geoffrey Waldon working with children as well as conversations with people attending his workshops, about his theories of child development.

3
EARLY COGNITIVE DEVELOPMENT

This chapter explains how a child's general understanding develops and describes the essential abilities that make this happen. The growth in general understanding can be visualised as a tree. The trunk is the foundation, it must be strong and solid to carry all the branches that represent the richness of human skills and abilities.

When a baby picks up a toy and explores it with his hands or puts it in his mouth, he is learning something about the world around him; his physical skills enable him to interact with the environment. Layer upon layer of experience build the foundations for the cognitive abilities which enable him to process information, solve problems and learn, and it all starts with the movement abilities.

Geoffrey Waldon described the continuum of development, and as previously mentioned, I have devised a structure to represent this growth in general understanding. There are three significant developmental levels which roughly correspond to the first three years of life:

Level 1: Early movement abilities develop during the first year.

Level 2: Continuant capacity emerges in the second year; this is the ability to think and plan sequences of movements with objects.

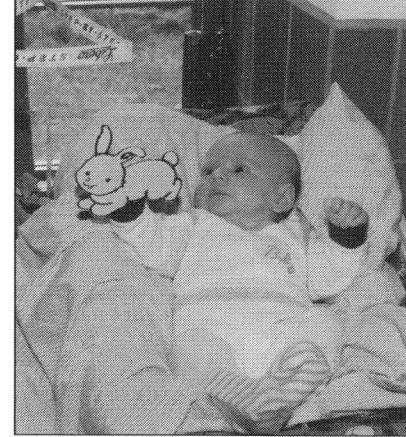

Level 3: The learning to learn capacities are the mental processes for organising and using experiences; these develop from the third year and continue to grow throughout life.

Waldon defined six capacities:

- Matching
- Sorting
- Seriation
- Drawing
- Brick-building
- Coding

Each capacity is subdivided into three stages, ***early***, ***active*** and ***mature***. Each stage corresponds to approximately 12 months of development.

SECTION 1: BACKGROUND AND THEORY

The development of understanding

The crown with its many branches, twigs and leaves, represents the expansion of the learning capacities and the richness of understanding.

LEVEL 3

Branching out is the growing capacity to remember and make choices during self-directed play.

LEVEL 2

The strong trunk is the child's well-integrated body and motivation to explore.

LEVEL 1

Everything new he learns, grows out of what he has learned before and contains the essence of what has gone before. Therefore, the more soundly anything is understood, the richer and more varied the state of understanding, the more probable it is to prove the source and foundation of wide-ranging and mature abilities in the future.

DR GEOFFREY WALDON UNDERSTANDING UNDERSTANDING 1980

Level 1. Developments in the first year: Fundamental movement abilities

Let us take a closer look at the specific movement abilities listed on the trunk; these are all essential for interacting with the physical world, for touching and handling objects and for the child's ability to explore with purpose and intent.

Key skill: Effortful movement
From birth:

When the baby is awake, his body is active. He is born with an inclination to move; his arms wave and his legs kick about. It is through this constant movement of the limbs that the baby becomes aware of his body and also familiar with the space around him. As the baby grows, his movements become more effortful, vigorous and varied, and the more effortful he is, the more he discovers.

Key skill: Bodily integration
Around 14 weeks:

The infant's body becomes integrated. This means the baby has a growing awareness that each limb is part of his body and he can move them separately or together. The integration happens as the arms and legs accidentally come into contact with one another as they explore the same bodily space.

The baby begins to understand where each limb is in space and he learns to control the direction and the focus of the movements. At this stage, the baby is also very interested in his hands and his ability to hold and manipulate small objects grows rapidly from now on.

Key skill: Focusing interest and acting on the surroundings
By 6–7 months:

By this age the baby is getting more upright, he learns to sit with support and this gives him a new view of the space around him. He can focus his interest on a toy close to him and reach out to pick it up. However, if he becomes interested in something else, he automatically drops the first toy as if he has forgotten he is holding it. In the early stages, a baby turns his whole body towards the toy he wants and in so doing, he may topple over as he reaches out.

The ability to reach and cross the midline with the hands is an important developmental skill which emerges around this stage. The midline is an imaginary line running down the middle of the child, with the right side and the left side as two separate entities. The child must be able to reach across this line and use both hands with confidence in all the spaces around him, this is important for full bodily integration, the development of hand dominance and also the ability to track an object with the eyes.

Key skill: Picking up and exploring objects
7 months onward:

As the baby's core becomes stronger, he learns to sit unsupported and he is stable enough to reach out and pick up toys without losing balance. He is learning to judge how far he can reach and this ability grows stronger through the constant effort of trying. Babies start to crawl around this age and their curiosity in exploring objects pushes them to reach further and also to move towards the objects that catch their eye.

When the baby manipulates a toy in his hands, he experiences it in several ways: the form, weight, texture, smell and taste. He may also discover what he can do with it: take, for example, the baby who accidentally strikes a block against the table-top and it makes a noise; this accidental discovery leads him to repeat the movement to create the sound again. By nine months, the baby has discovered banging, be it a spoon on the table or two blocks together; he likes the noise and he knows how to do it. Waldon referred to this action as **banging and scraping behaviour**; it is an important developmental step because it signifies the beginning of tool-use.

Key skill: Making choices and planning actions

11 months onward:

The baby looks around for things to explore and now he takes time to investigate the toys. He sees a yogurt pot, he picks it up and turns it over; a brick falls out, it just happened to be inside.

He notices this brick and he decides to put it back in the pot, but now he tips it out on purpose. A new game has evolved: the game of **picking up and putting in**. The baby repeats the picking up and putting in action again and again; it's great fun! Then something new happens, this time the brick lands on a little car instead of the carpet, and that makes a very different sound; the baby notices this and he does it again. The baby takes the game a step further when the car becomes part of his game: he puts the car into the yogurt pot and tips it out. The game has expanded from repeating a familiar action and in the process, something unexpected happened and the baby has learnt something new.

The baby begins to plan and make definite choices about which toy to pick up. As he reaches out for the chosen one, he is no longer distracted by the other toys in the path; he knows what he wants. At this stage he continues to play picking up and putting in games but he uses a range of containers, he chooses where to put all the different bits: some go in the posting box and others on the back of the lorry.

This behaviour is indicative of the emergence of a new mental capacity which involves planning the actions and choosing the toys; the child can think about what to pick up from a collection, where to put it given several options, and he may also change his mind during this process. The technical term for this capacity is Early Inertial Memory and it is a critical development which emerges from the picking up and putting in games.

In summary, the bodily integration and the movement abilities which develop in the first year of life build the essential foundation for the child's ability to actively explore; these are the first learning to learn abilities.

> ### *Harry*
>
> Harry was always clutching a brick in one hand and twiddling his fingers on the other. He spent a lot of time just staring, holding the brick tight and twiddling. He did not explore and he seemed afraid of reaching out into the world around him.
>
> With gentle guidance, Harry began to engage in picking up and putting in activities. Initially he used only one hand at a time, he wasn't ready to let go of his brick. Gradually he learnt to reach out and this helped him to focus on a point away from his own narrow world and he became familiar with the space around him; he discovered how to explore with his hands. Harry watched the toys drop into the box and he started to repeat the game on his own. Before long, he became less attached to his brick, and he put it down in order to use both hands; Harry posted wooden discs into a tall container and he enjoyed filling an empty chocolate box with walnuts. Harry was now focusing his attention on the objects around him and learning what he could do with them; he had discovered how interesting the world could be.

Level 2. Developments in the second year: The continuant capacity

Geoffrey Waldon observed and described a behaviour which emerges in the second year, the continuant capacity, defined as:

> *The ability to remember and to choose between objects and to move them from place to place in sequence and to keep going.*

Waldon named this ability continuant behaviour or continuant capacity; the latter term will be used here. The ability starts to emerge around 14 months: it grows out of picking up and putting in, which is the characteristic behaviour at the end of the first year. However, the play now changes from random exploration of the objects and it becomes very purposeful: the objects are moved around in a planned and deliberate fashion from place to place. The child continues this activity for long periods of time, he keeps moving objects around, organising and reorganising; this is continuant capacity behaviour.

When we analyse in more detail the levels of understanding required to carry out these activities, it becomes apparent how essential the continuant capacity is for learning.

- ▶ The child can **choose what to focus on** and he can ignore other things; for example, he can choose to pick up the blocks and he will not get distracted by the cars.
- ▶ The child can **keep going and repeat an action** several times over, e.g. move the water bottles one by one from the box in the corner to the table in the centre of the room.
- ▶ The child can **make the choice** of where to put the object, put on the shelf or behind the chair.
- ▶ The child can **carry out a movement sequence**. This can be simple or more complex with several steps; the child might change his original plan during the course of moving the toys around. One example goes as follows: first arrange all the cars in one long line at the edge of the carpet, then the next move is to create a queue with all the trucks near the sofa and put the rest on the window sill.

- ▶ The child can **imagine a sequence of events** such as 'I'll put this ball in the toy box and then I will push the truck to the door and then...'
- ▶ The child can **retain a mental image** of an activity when he is no longer doing it, for example he can remember where he left a stone and how to drop it into the paddling pool.

These play activities are characteristic of children between the ages of 14 and 30 months, and the emergence coincides with the time when children usually learn to walk independently. That gives them the freedom to carry and move things in a wider space: to think, plan and make their own choices.

Here is an example of a child engaged in a continuant capacity activity. He is in the garden with Dad who is raking leaves; the toddler is playing alongside, absorbed in his own game:

- ▶ The child picks up some stones, he bangs them on the paving;
- ▶ He drops them deliberately then picks them up and puts them into a bucket;
- ▶ He walks across the lawn and tips the stones out by the tree;
- ▶ He goes back to the flowerbed to pick up a stick, he decides to look for another stick;
- ▶ He holds them together;
- ▶ He decides to poke the two sticks into the ground next to each other.

...and the game carries on. The toddler is exploring the materials, arranging and grouping the objects together and later reorganising everything; through doing he is noticing how the objects behave in different ways.

This stage is quite literally the **carrier phase** for learning; the child is thinking and planning what to do next and he is able to consciously change his mind, he is effortful and engrossed. This type of play is non-directed, there is no right nor wrong; the child is exploring for its own sake and he does not have an end-point in mind, the activity is on-going.

The adults around might talk to him and comment, they might tell him what the things are called or what they can do; but his actual understanding comes from playing, his understanding of the language associated with the activities is acquired later.

In summary, the continuant capacity is the second essential tool for learning; it involves movement, memory, planning, sequencing and choice. Anything that interferes with its development is going to cause problems with the acquisition of the learning to learn capacities at the next level.

Level 3. Developments in the third year: The learning to learn capacities

By the third year of life, the **learning to learn trunk** is strong and the **branches** start to grow; these branches are the general cognitive capacities used to analyse and organise our understanding of the world. Geoffrey Waldon chose the term **learning to learn tools**; in this book the term **learning to learn capacities** is used, in order to clarify that the abilities are mental capacities, not physical tools. These general cognitive capacities can be defined as six distinct but closely interconnected learning capacities; they develop simultaneously from the third year onwards. Here is a brief description of each of the six capacities.

Matching

This is the concept that two things go together to make a pair because they are similar but not necessarily identical. Imagine you have broken one of your favourite mugs; you go looking in the shops to find one to match, but the manufacturer has changed the glaze, so you settle for a new mug which is only ever so slightly different from the old one; it is good enough to be a match.

Sorting

As the child explores, he becomes aware of similarities between objects; he begins to group things together as he notices common features. For example some objects may feel rough, some roll and others have corners etc. He might discover that long objects are good for prodding and stick them all in the sand together; stones and shells are both hard but different and he decides to collect them into two separate buckets. Sorting is the beginning of classification.

Seriation or sequencing

The human brain is primed to look for patterns and order and one aspect of this is understanding series. There are two types of series, firstly the **repeating pattern sequence** such as (red, blue, green), (red, blue, green). The second type is the **expansive series**, which is concerned with understanding order according to size, for example stacking cups or Russian dolls.

Drawing

The skill of drawing grows out of the ability to control the movements of the arms, combined with the ability to hold an object in the hand. The child becomes aware that he can create a noise by banging a toy; later he notices the marks made when he moves the tool over a surface, for example in the sand pit or on his dinner plate. The marks, lines and scribbles will in time become drawings that represent the world and writing later becomes a means of conveying meaning.

Brick-building

This is the ability to understand the spatial and functional relationship between objects. A child is sitting by himself and creating a pile with objects, one keeps falling off, he puts it back, it falls again and again, then he places it differently and nothing happens, it stays! He begins to understand how to place the objects in relation to each other: he becomes aware of their orientation, the distance between them, their relative size etc., all aspects to consider to create a stable model.

SECTION I: BACKGROUND AND THEORY

Coding

This is the capacity to associate signs or symbols in an arbitrary way. Take, for example, this outline: ✋; there are many different meanings to this symbol. ✋ can mean a hand, in another context ✋ = 5, ✋ = STOP or even ✋ = Goodbye. This concept leads to the understanding and use of conventional symbols, for example in reading and numeracy, road signs or washing labels.

Growth of the learning to learn capacities

Geoffrey Waldon used the phrase **'First we learn to sort and then we sort to learn'** which applies to all the six learning capacities. The child gradually acquires a set of mental tools to process and organise his experiences and when these capacities are fully developed, they become his active tools for learning. At the early stages the child's learning is always through his practical experiences but in time, he can think about a problem and work it out in his head.

The gradual development of the six mental capacities can be observed in the child's general approach to novel tasks and how effectively he can use new experiences. In general, by the end of the third year, the child can make pairs (**matching**), he will attempt to copy patterns either drawn (**drawing**) or using bricks (**brick-building**), he will search for similarities and differences (**sorting**) and he can look for repeated sequences (**seriation**).

Around the age of 4½, there is an important new development: the child can actively apply his learning to learn capacities to acquire specific skills. Take, for example, reading, it is essential to be able to match letters, to perceive and remember a sequence and to be able to decode a string of letters as well as having the drawing skills to copy patterns and write by hand. In order to understand numbers, the child must be able to match patterns, sort objects into groups, understand an expansive series, record numbers in writing and decode the numerals as symbols, for example 5 means ●●●●●.

In summary, the learning to learn capacities are the higher-level mental processing tools which we need to generate meaning from our experiences; these are fully embedded when the child has moved through the **early** and **active stages** to reach the stage of **mature abilities**; he now has all the tools for learning. These are all described in full in chapter 9.

Albert

Albert had lots of special interests and he was good at occupying himself; he liked to line up his toys around the classroom and he also enjoyed building complicated Lego models. However, when the teacher asked him to do some work with her, he often ran away.

She changed her approach; she arranged some sorting boards on the table and she started to sort some patterned cards into several sets, working quietly on her own. Every now and again, she went over to Albert and gave him a card; before long he joined her at the table, and he began to sort the cards. The teacher gradually withdrew and Albert continued on his own.

Too many verbal instructions confused Albert and he didn't understand them; he had learnt how to avoid a situation by running off. When he was shown what to do, he could make sense and join in. The great variety of non-verbal activities became the platform for his engagement in new learning experiences.

The importance of hand-held tools

Tool-use develops alongside the other learning to learn abilities and it is an integral part of the learning experiences at all levels.

The human hand is the most amazing tool in itself and it enables us to carry out intricate and complex tasks. It is an unspecialised tool but with practice, the thumb and the fingers can work skilfully together and we can quite literally turn our hands to anything! The controlled movements of the arm and the skill of the hand are closely integrated abilities and they develop together. When we can hold an object in the hand and use it with purpose, the object becomes a tool. Geoffrey Waldon defined a tool as 'an object which somehow extends the abilities of the user... conferring the possibilities for novel skill'.

The essence is to discover and understand the potential of an object, how it can be used to solve a problem. The child might discover that he can retrieve a ball from under the settee with a stick, or if he climbs onto a chair, he can reach the sweetie jar on the fridge; the stick and the chair have become tools. They helped him to achieve something that was previously impossible.

For human beings, tools play a vital role in life; they are used to make many everyday tasks easier or even possible. This may be using a spatula to turn the sausages on the pan without burning the fingers, using a hedge trimmer, a pair of scissors, a drumstick on the drum... the list carries on. The many conventional tools require specific skills to be mastered. However, the focus here is firmly on developing and practising the underlying movement abilities and dexterity. The ideas for practical activities can be found in section 3.

LEARNING DIFFICULTIES AND THE IMPACT ON THE ABILITY TO LEARN

The term learning difficulties, is used here to describe children who experience obstacles to learning. The nature and the origins of these obstacles can be many and varied and the impact of the difficulty will be individual to the child.

We know that the development of general understanding follows a universal path for all children. Through effortful activities and with their ***experience gathering equipment***, they learn how to learn and develop an understanding of the world; the body and the mind develop together at an evenly matched pace. Unfortunately for children with a learning difficulty, this is rarely the case, and what you see is a discrepancy between their understanding, their physical development and their social and emotional maturity; this disharmony has a significant impact on all aspects of their development.

Insecure foundations for learning

Movement abilities and effort are essential for learning and for that reason the growth of the early fundamental movement abilities is critical. Many children with learning difficulties tend to be less active and have a much narrower range of activities in which they engage. This will have a significant impact on their early learning: it can result in poor bodily integration, which in turn leads to a fragmented understanding of the space around the body, a lack of coordination and an impaired ability to maintain focus and interest in activities. The children will struggle to stay engaged for extended periods of time which leads to a decrease in the learning opportunities. Take, for example, a child who is poorly coordinated: he will struggle with picking up objects, manipulating and moving them around. He will find it challenging to use his hands together to open a box and take out the toys or to hold a bucket and fill it with sand; he will be doing less and therefore learning less.

Some children also develop what can be termed ***effort-saving habits***, such as the child who is leaning on one arm whilst the other does the 'work'. This behaviour may be caused by poor integration, lack of coordination and weak core stability; putting in effort can feel too exhausting and the child ends up expending as little effort as possible to complete the task. All the short-cuts will limit the range of his experiences and this becomes a vicious cycle: less effort means fewer experiences, which in turn means less growth in understanding. This highlights the need for continued effortful activities: children need to be active to learn.

Some children can become stuck in repetitive and restrictive patterns of behaviour. They enjoy very specific tasks and repeat them over and over. Take, for example, the child who spends his time lining up bricks with absolute precision or another child who likes to tie pieces of strings together. They are very specialised behaviours and the children become very skilled at doing them. However, by their repetitive nature and with no variations, they become restrictive and limiting. These children can feel challenged when they are encouraged to broaden out and participate in a much wider range of activities. The unfamiliarity can cause anxiety.

It is pertinent at this point to refer back to the model of development with the tree trunk as the foundation and the branches the higher-level cognitive capacities. Some children do develop very specialised higher-level skills and these can be very impressive; however, some of these skills can be likened to small twigs, or splinter skills, without a sound foundation and no application in real life. This is seen with some children on the autism spectrum; take for example the girl who can recall everyone's birthday after she has been told just once, but she is unable to work out how old a person is. Another example is the boy who can detect the smallest variation in the colours of crayons and he gets very distressed when a crayon is not exactly right; he does not have the ability to think about the problem, to work out how to look for another box of crayons nor the ability to compare two colours side by side to find the one he desires.

 Note

> - Start at the child's developmental level, not his chronological age.
> - Build and strengthen the foundations before moving on to the next level.
> - Every child is different, every one an individual: always be flexible, adapt and adjust.

Autism and learning

Autism is a specific learning difficulty which affects social interaction and communication as well as sensory integration. The autism spectrum is a wide umbrella of abilities and difficulties: some have high levels of cognitive abilities whereas others function at a relatively low level, they may be non-verbal and socially remote. There is a wealth of information available elsewhere which describes in detail the autism spectrum condition; in the present context, the focus is on the impact on the development of the learning to learn abilities.

Children with autism often have insecure body and spatial awareness which can stem from an underlying sensory integration difficulty. The children may limit their movements and the space they explore, they can be reluctant to touch and manipulate objects in their hands. These children may develop a limited repertoire of movements and they frequently get stuck in repetitive behaviours with which they are familiar and feel comfortable. It is essential to go back to basics and encourage the development of the early movement abilities so the children become comfortable with the full range of movements they need to create new experiences.

It is well known that the social aspect of learning is a challenge for children with autism: they struggle to make sense of people, to understand their intentions or the implied meanings in what is said or done; these children find it much easier to concentrate on the cognitive tasks if the social interaction is kept to a minimum, thereby limiting the amount of information they have to process.

Delay in language development is common in these children, and there is often a discrepancy between their cognitive and language levels. Teaching through verbal explanations may not be appropriate: a lengthy verbal description may at best be lost on the child but it can at worst cause confusion and anxiety. The non-social lesson format is ideal: it builds understanding through doing, it removes both the need to process language and the distraction of the social interaction whilst learning.

Language, communication and interaction

Children need their parents and teachers to interact with them to develop their language and communication skills, the essential ingredients for building social relationships; the adults need to be emotionally present and attentive to the child for this to happen. This should occupy substantial parts of every child's day. The other strand of development is the growth in cognition, and we have seen that this grows through active exploration in the early years. The child is learning through doing, usually without the adults being actively involved.

Many children with special needs have difficulties in both areas of development, and they obviously need a well-balanced curriculum. This book addresses one strand, cognitive development, and it should be complemented by relationship-based interventions which encourage the development of communication and social understanding; information about these approaches can be found elsewhere.

Emotion and learning

The child's emotional response to the challenges of learning is important. Take a child faced with a new activity: if he thinks it is too difficult or he doesn't understand, he will feel challenged and this can cause anxiety; an anxious child cannot learn. The uncomfortable feelings give rise to a physical response, this can be:

- ▶ *Fight*, which is manifested in such behaviours as throwing stuff, hitting or biting the adult.
- ▶ *Flight*, when the child tries to get away.
- ▶ *Freeze*, as seen when the child becomes passive or resistant.

These behaviours prevent the child from getting involved and it takes careful management of the learning situation to provide him with experiences which make him feel good and capable.

Some children are emotionally volatile and they cannot cope with feelings of perceived failure. A child might unintentionally knock a tower down or drop a bead on the floor: these are accidents but they can cause enormous distress. The child might feel a failure and be unable to manage the strong feelings evoked. The activities in this programme can help some children who are emotionally fragile. They can learn to deal with the unexpected through carefully selected games. For example, introducing variations moves them from the familiar to the unfamiliar; making piles involves creating stacks of objects without an underlying structure and everything can move, roll or collapse. Such experiences provide a safe way to build resilience.

There are many sources with much more detailed information about the development of emotional maturity; in this context, suffice it to say, that attunement to the child's feelings and having the ability to create a learning environment free from fear of failure, is vital.

> ### Zoe (1)
>
> Zoe loved scooping small cubes from one bowl into another. This calls for effort, coordination and motor planning. When she accidentally dropped a cube, her reactions appeared extreme; she screamed and she swiped everything off the table.
>
> But she didn't do anything wrong, there is no right or wrong in this activity. She just dropped a cube and that happens when you are practising a new skill. But Zoe felt that she had made a mistake and she could not tolerate that.

Challenging behaviours

Waldon talked about primary and secondary impediments to learning; the primary impediment refers to a diagnosed syndrome such as autism or another specific disorder, which have known or predictable effects on the child's development. On the other hand, the secondary impediments are the behaviours which the child produces, and these behaviours can become great obstacles to their development. Waldon referred to these behaviours as 'handicap behaviours', using the terminology of the time; he made the point that when a child behaves in this way, he prevents himself from learning and making progress; he gets himself stuck and he does not move on.

There are many different 'handicap behaviours' a child might use, and these are similar to the fight, flight and freeze reactions described above, for example:

- Refusing to participate with a *no, no, no!*
- Sliding under the table and trying to get away.
- Hurting the adult in some way: biting, scratching, hitting or throwing his head backwards.
- Extreme passivity: this can be going limp or totally rigid, either way the child does not participate.
- Turning his head and eye-gaze away.
- Crying and screaming.
- Throwing the equipment or deliberately breaking it.

Most children will resort to some of these behaviours at some point even if the tasks are well within their cognitive abilities. There are several reasons why that happens:

- In the early days this method of working together is unfamiliar to him.
- He may *feel* it is too difficult and he doesn't understand.
- He is unused to the effort which is required of him.
- He may be emotionally volatile and he cannot yet cope with even the smallest challenge.
- He might be highly sensitive to environmental distractions such as noise, movement or light.
- He might have a repertoire of learnt, habitual responses he resorts to whenever a demand is made.

Let us meet Zoe again to consider what triggered her behaviour; during the previous incident we saw her as being emotionally volatile: she felt she was failing. Here is another situation.

> ### Zoe (2)
>
> Zoe loves threading curtain rings onto a kitchen roll stand. She is fully engaged until something disturbs her concentration: she hears a noise and she sees someone walk past. Once again, she swipes all the equipment off the table but this time she laughs out loud. There are two reasons for this behaviour: firstly, Zoe is very sensitive to visual and auditory distractions such as someone walking past, and that triggered the instant response of clearing everything off the table; secondly, she has learnt that this behaviour often gets a reaction from people and she really enjoys their attention. She has learnt that throwing stuff can be very entertaining!

Zoe's behaviours can be described as 'handicap behaviours' as they impacted hugely on her learning: after swiping the table clear there was nothing left to play with. The causes of her behaviour need to be understood and they fell into the categories of emotional volatility, extreme sensitivity to environmental distractions as well as learnt, habitual responses. A new programme was needed for Zoe which was designed to address these underlying causes and help her to move on developmentally. The following elements were incorporated into her programme of intervention:

- Zoe was engaged in a daily learning to learn session lasting up to half an hour.
- She practised lots of movement-based activities such as piling, posting and scooping; this helped to improve her motor skills and increased her confidence.
- Initially she worked in a quiet space; in time, distractions were introduced. This helped to increase her tolerance of noise and the presence of other people.
- Lots of variations were incorporated to create new experiences at the same level, giving her a broader base of general understanding.
- No one responded when she threw the toys on the floor; there were no reprimands nor requests to pick up what she had thrown.
- The adult ensured that every activity could continue uninterrupted; if she threw the equipment the facilitator was prepared and she always had a similar activity within reach.

> ### Zoe (3)
>
> As Zoe grew in confidence her engagement and tolerance improved greatly; she stopped throwing the toys and she could work in the classroom with the other children. In time, she became more mature and she spontaneously started to tidy up at the end of the session; in her mind, this became an integral part of the lesson. Zoe gradually learnt to regulate her emotions and she was able to think, 'OK, I dropped something, never mind, I'll try again, it is not the end of the world!'

How to respond to challenging behaviours

The structured learning environment is designed to make the child feel secure, thus enabling him to participate in familiar activities within his comfort zone; they are chosen to strengthen his learning abilities without making him feel pressured or challenged. If the child still displays challenging behaviours, reassess the difficulty of the task, lower the demands or change the activity. At the same time, deal with the behaviours themselves in a very low-key fashion:

- Do not reprimand or correct the child.
- Pay no attention to the behaviours.
- Keep the session flowing and carry on.
- Adjust the demands and do something simpler.

Further practical advice for dealing with specific challenging behaviours during the working session, is given in chapter 5.

Scott is very impulsive, he tends to throw everything in sight, as can be seen here: the toys are scattered all over the floor. But Scott also thrives on structure, and he can concentrate on simple, ordered activities for long periods of time; they create order in his mind.

SECTION 2: IMPLEMENTATION

Introduction

This section has two chapters:

Chapter 5:

This contains a description of the non-verbal approach with detailed instructions of how to work with the child. It sets out the 'how to do it' and it should provide all the information needed to get started at home or in school.

Chapter 6:

This chapter provides a thorough explanation of how to carry out an initial assessment together with a developmental framework to record and track the child's learning to learn abilities.

5
THE PRACTICAL IMPLEMENTATION OF THE LEARNING TO LEARN APPROACH

The key principles of the learning to learn session:

- ▶ The session simulates the non-social play of a young child, sitting by himself and playing with his toys.
- ▶ The adult is a facilitator. She helps the child to become and stay engrossed.
- ▶ The activities are designed to develop early cognitive abilities.
- ▶ There are no social demands made on the child; the adult doesn't talk, explain or give praise whilst they are working together.
- ▶ The adult does not reprimand the child or comment on his behaviour.
- ▶ The facilitator initially sits behind the child and guides him with hand over hand, to get him involved in the activities.
- ▶ There is no overt skills training in the session. For example, the child is not taught to tie shoe laces, cut out a circle, tidy up, count to five etc. The focus is always on the child's general, underlying abilities.
- ▶ All activities are based on previous experiences with added variations within the child's current level of understanding.
- ▶ The child should be enjoying the activities.

During the working session there is a feeling of togetherness, despite the absence of verbal communication. The adult must be emotionally present because this will make the child feel safe when he encounters new learning challenges.

When children are introduced to this non-verbal way of working, it may at first seem rather strange: they are used to the teacher talking to them. This is different and, like any other new situation, it takes time to get used to the change; once they are familiar with the format, they thoroughly enjoy it: it is quiet and they can concentrate and become fully absorbed.

It is quite common for children to resort to some challenging behaviours during the initial teaching sessions; they are likely to feel a bit uncertain because of the change in the teacher's way of teaching. They might use a variety of behaviours such resisting and hiding their hands or they start to throw the equipment around, they may slide off the chair and some decide to make a lot of noise. These avoidance behaviours rarely persist for long because the children experience the pleasures of **doing** and the feelings of being capable. Pay no attention to the behaviours, instead continue playing as if nothing untoward has happened; dealing with challenging behaviours is covered in more detail later.

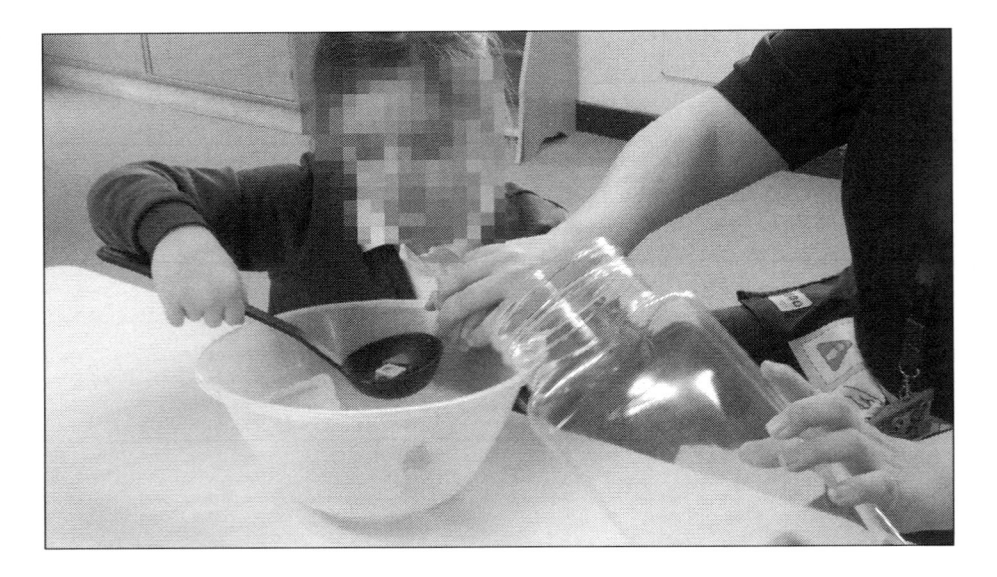

General advice on using the approach

- ▶ All sessions start with effortful 'picking up and putting in' activities, whatever the child's current cognitive level. These activities will energise the child and encourage his sustained attention; the familiar tasks add to the enjoyment and the sense of competence.
- ▶ The length of a session is flexible, but the longer the better! If the time is short, keep the focus on strengthening the fundamental skills.
- ▶ The ethos is to play in the way of a young child and at the early stages he does not seek to 'finish'. For that reason, try to avoid finishing i.e. don't pick up everything, but instead restart the game whilst there are still objects left on the table. This can also encourage more flexibility and tolerance and avoid the fixation on closure which some children have.
- ▶ Introduce the next activity before clearing away the previous activity; this promotes the sense of no fixed end-goal; the play should be ongoing though constantly changing.
- ▶ When children play by themselves, they use their toys in many different ways. Adults are often surprised by their flexible thinking: bricks can be used to build towers, be cars in a carpark, a line of shops or sheep in a field. The same goes for the learning to learn session: every piece of equipment has many potential uses and should be incorporated into lots of different activities.

How to keep the child engaged

Throughout most sessions, there is a natural ebb and flow, some games will immediately capture the child and he becomes totally involved; at other times an activity doesn't work so well. The game might have too many steps, the manipulative skills are too taxing, the sequence is too complicated and so on. Always start from the premise that the child is struggling because he doesn't yet understand or he hasn't got the skills; analyse the situation and consider how the game can be adjusted or changed to suit his level.

Increase support. Sometimes a child might not perceive and follow the pattern intended by the adult. The first intervention is to increase support: this can be hand over hand guidance or a simple point, 'This is where it goes!'

Readjust the cognitive demands. It might become clear that the activity is beyond the child's current level of understanding. Take as an example the activity to separate into sets a collection of shells, bottle tops and buttons: if the child places the objects at random into the sorting trays, he is clearly not yet ready for sorting. Make a change:

- Use the equipment in a different and less demanding way: turn the sorting activity into a posting game. Give the child a cardboard tube and demonstrate how to drop everything through the tube into a flowerpot; this will re-engage him and he will have a new experience of posting through a tube.
- Introduce a large spoon and the sorting game becomes a tool use activity, scooping all the bits and pieces into a bucket.

The activities are essentially the same as far as the child is aware, but the demands on his understanding have been subtly lowered; he is not sensing any failure.

Getting started

Equipment

The vast majority of the equipment used in this programme is multi-functional: that means it can be used to practise many different skills and abilities at several levels. The equipment tends to be quite simple and some will already exist in the classroom or at home; other items can be collected, 'loose bits' which have no real purpose such as lids, empty egg boxes etc. Do ensure they meet the required safety standards.

Some toys and equipment are designed to work on very specific skills. Take, for example, an inset board with three shapes: this will train the child to place the three shapes in the correct holes, but it does not develop a deeper understanding of shapes. The learning to learn programme rarely incorporates such toys into the activities. Instead the recommendation is to collect material which is multi-functional and can be adapted and used in many games.

Object collections

- Collect sets of objects with different feel in weight, texture, size etc., for example bricks, fir cones, bean bags, potatoes, buttons, straws, curtain rings, bangles, bottle tops, clothes pegs, keys, lids etc.
- Make collections of objects with similar characteristics like a pile of corks, different types of clothes pegs, round discs in different materials; these collections are useful for sorting.
- Consider the size of the objects in relation to the child's hands: weighty objects are good as they give more sensory feedback and are great for posting and placing; smaller objects are useful to practise dexterity. It is harder to find objects that are appropriate for older children in terms of size and weight, and homemade alternatives may be needed.
- Avoid using objects which are also pretend toys; a set of animals can be used for sorting but the child is likely to start an imaginative game and, in this context, the symbolic play is a distraction.

Containers

- Gather a set of containers in various shapes and sizes: ice-cream tubs, bowls, jugs, buckets, plastic trays, saucepans, baking tins, flower pots, muffin tins and a kitchen roll stand can 'hold' things like curtain rings – use whatever is available.

Tools

▶ Tools can be large or small, light or heavy; it is good to have a varied assortment. Many everyday utensils can be used such as scoops, large spoons, rolling pins, strong cardboard tubes, BBQ tongs, sugar tongs, a 40–50 cm long piece of dowelling, chop sticks etc.

Specialised Waldon equipment

Geoffrey Waldon designed a range of equipment with multiple uses. They are made primarily in wood to make them sturdy and give them weight. These are expensive to purchase and it is possible to substitute some of them by adapting the use of everyday items.

The boat

This is referred to as 'the boat' or 'wooden boat' with pegs or peg people. It consists of two identical halves with holes and large pegs. It is used, among other things, for spatial awareness, sequencing and continuant capacity activities.

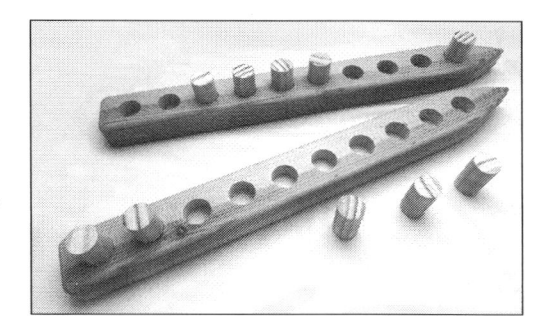

H-board

The name is a simple reference to the H-shaped divisions on the board. It is used for playing pairing and matching games, as well as ordering and sequencing.

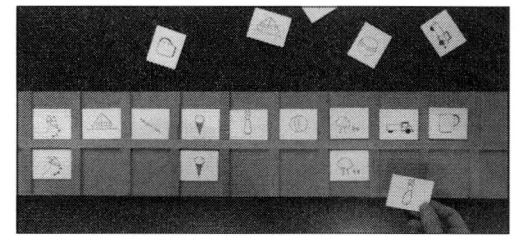

Pegboard

This pegboard is used to practise spatial awareness, sequencing and patterns. The pegs can also be used for putting in, lining up, creating small groups etc.

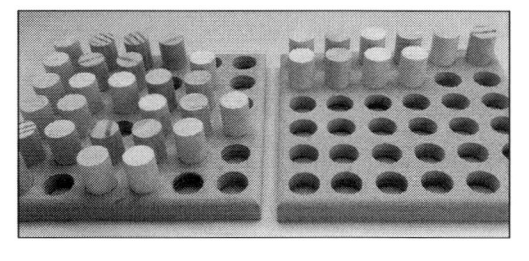

SECTION 2: IMPLEMENTATION

Sorting boards

Sorting boards are designed for sorting cards into categories. They can also be used for continuant capacity games, making patterns and sequences. The dividers on the boards are narrow strips of woods which has the advantage of creating defined spaces and preventing the cards from sliding around. Similar boards can be made from foam board with non-slip pads on the back.

Hollow bricks

These hollow bricks are used for eye-hand coordination and spatial awareness activities. They can be moved with a stick and also incorporated into sequencing activities by placing smaller objects inside them.

There is a list with suggestions for equipment in the appendix as well as a more detailed description of the specialised Waldon equipment.

Organising the classroom and the work areas

The working space is simply a table and two chairs with the equipment nearby. This can be in a corner of the classroom or in a separate room if the child is very distractible.

Think about the space around the table as part of the working area as it provides opportunities for reaching out into the wider body space. The working area can be extended by placing a second table at an angle or chairs next to the child's seat on which containers can be placed.

In order to make the child feel well-balanced, his chair and the table must be at the correct height, his feet should be flat on the floor (or on a box); they should not dangle as that affects his core stability. The table is at the right height when his lower arms can rest comfortably on it.

The sessions are usually conducted one to one but it is possible to have several separate sessions taking place at the same time within the classroom; this is indeed to be encouraged, as it creates an atmosphere conducive to learning for everyone.

The reality of the classroom is that a member of staff often has to support several children at the same time. It is possible to arrange a session around one large table: some children will receive individual help whilst the rest have the opportunity to explore and play with the equipment on their own. The teacher should maintain her focus on one child at a time whilst keeping an eye on the activities around the table.

Try to arrange the play equipment so everything is within easy reach. This is to avoid getting up during the working session as that disrupts the flow and it has an unsettling effect.

A storage trolley with baskets is a great way to organise the equipment as it can be moved around to where it is needed. The baskets can be organised and labelled with the different types of equipment which makes it easy to use and share among staff.

How to give the child hand-over-hand support

Every child is different and there are no hard and fast rules about how to provide the physical support; the skill of the adult is in adjusting the help given to the child, always trying to ensure that the activity flows well and she maintains a good pace and rhythm that is comfortable and enjoyable for the child.

- ▶ Work hand over hand and help the child to pick up and dispose of the objects.
- ▶ Work hand over hand to create rhythmic picking up, alternating the hands for picking up.
- ▶ Reduce the prompt when the child is actively picking up by himself; now the support can be eased to holding the wrist or the underarm.
- ▶ The child's movements can be supported without touching his hands. One method is to hold one arm back and encourage a forward movement of the other hand, instilling a 'push forward, pull back'-motion; this can create a steady rhythm, alternating the use of the hands.
- ▶ Fade the prompt as soon as the child is able to continue the activity on his own; he can now pick up and place the items and keep going without support.
- ▶ The adult can demonstrate or point to show the child what to do; this is a suitable technique when the child has reached the developmental stage of attending to someone else's model and understanding how to copy.
- ▶ Be flexible in the support given. The child might be working without help for a while and then his attention falters; this is the time to step up the help with hand over hand guidance to get him back on track.
- ▶ It is important to find a pace which suits each child; some work fast, others are naturally slower.

Touch-sensitive children

It is essential to be aware that some children are very touch-sensitive and a physical prompt can be really unpleasant for them; that makes it necessary to find alternative ways to provide support. The facilitator has to be inventive because there is no fixed way to give support. The overriding aim is to find an effective way to engage every child. Here are some ideas.

- Hold onto the child's sleeve rather than his hands to encourage the flow of movements.
- Move his hands by supporting his palm instead of holding his hands.
- Lightly support him on the arm rather than the hands.
- Work alongside and show the child what to do.
- During tool-use activities such as scooping, both the adult and the child can hold the tool together without touching each other.

The structured session

Planning the content

The format of the session follows the stages of development, which means always starting with a consolidation of the fundamental movement abilities, followed by the continuant capacity activities and finishing with the higher-level learning to learn capacities.

LEVEL 1: FUNDAMENTAL MOVEMENT ABILITIES

- ***Being effortful:*** lots of picking up and putting in.
- ***Use and range of space:*** scanning and searching for objects, retrieving objects.
- ***Complementary use of hands:*** such as sweeping or scooping actions.
- ***Maintaining focus:*** staying engaged for prolonged periods, adapting to variations.

LEVEL 2: CONTINUANT CAPACITY

- ***Activities*** that involve the use of several sets of objects.
- ***Choosing and moving*** these objects from one place to another in order.

LEVEL 3: LEARNING TO LEARN CAPACITIES

- ***There are six learning to learn capacities:*** focus on one or maybe two within a single session, such as playing some matching games as well as practising drawing skills.

Balance of the lesson content

The amount of time allocated to the activities at each level will naturally depend on the child's stage of development. There is often a tendency to rush through the movement activities to get to the 'clever stuff' at the higher levels. However, the most important part of the lesson is to consolidate the foundations before moving up the ladder to the more advanced abilities. A well-balanced lesson for a child functioning predominantly at level 1, 2 or 3 will look like this:

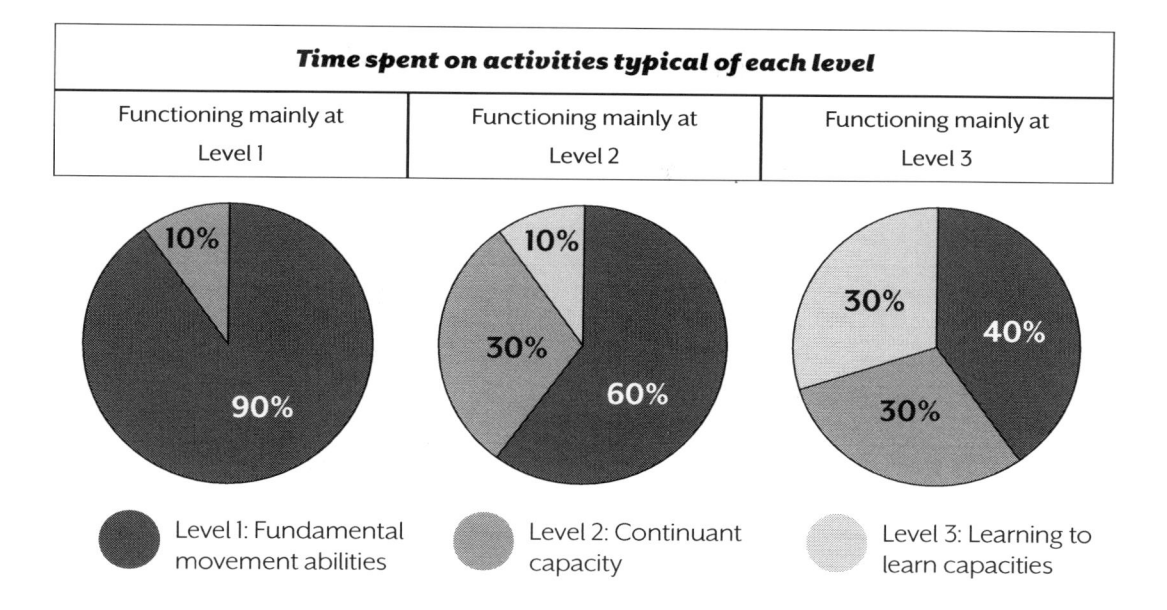

Time spent on activities typical of each level		
Functioning mainly at Level 1	Functioning mainly at Level 2	Functioning mainly at Level 3

- Level 1 pie chart: 90% Level 1, 10% Level 2
- Level 2 pie chart: 60% Level 1, 30% Level 2, 10% Level 3
- Level 3 pie chart: 40% Level 1, 30% Level 2, 30% Level 3

● Level 1: Fundamental movement abilities
● Level 2: Continuant capacity
● Level 3: Learning to learn capacities

Length of the session

▶ Each session should be as long as possible! It takes time to get mentally and physically 'warmed up' and become fully focused and ready to learn.

▶ The minimum length is about 20 minutes but children can keep going for much longer when the level is right for them, switching between easier and more advanced challenges throughout; 45 minutes to an hour is not unusual.

▶ Aim for several sessions a week, some short and some longer.

How to extend familiar activities with variations

Children always return to the activities they know, which is why familiar activities are the natural starting point; it makes them feel safe and confident as they know what to do. After a confident start, the facilitator can gradually introduce variations, each of these will become a new experience and learning opportunity. There are many ways to incorporate variations, and with experience, the facilitator will become skilled at seeing new possibilities.

Here are some suggestions:

▶ Practise the **same skills** with many **different objects**. Take, for example, 'picking up and putting in' games; these can be played with bricks, buttons, straws, bean bags, potatoes and they can be put into boxes, trays, jars, jugs, buckets and so on.

▶ Practise **different skills** using the **same equipment**. Think about the blocks, they are used for 'putting in', they can also be arranged in long lines which leads to sequencing, or picked up with a spoon which is a tool-use skill, as well as piled up high, the first step towards understanding three-dimensional space.

SECTION 2: IMPLEMENTATION

▶ **'Picking up and putting in' games can be varied in numerous ways:**
- ▶ The adult delivers one object at a time.
- ▶ The child picks up everything from a central pool.
- ▶ The objects are presented in different locations on the table: by the side, on the floor, held up next to the child, behind him or in front.
- ▶ The adult changes the speed of the delivery, fast and slow.
- ▶ The number of objects delivered at a time is increased, not just one, but several.
- ▶ Use a mixed collection of bits and pieces.
- ▶ Increase the number of containers on the table.
- ▶ Use a variety of containers: tall, wide, narrow, transparent etc.
- ▶ Place an obstacle in the way: put a cup over the cork and now the child must remove the cup in order to retrieve the cork.

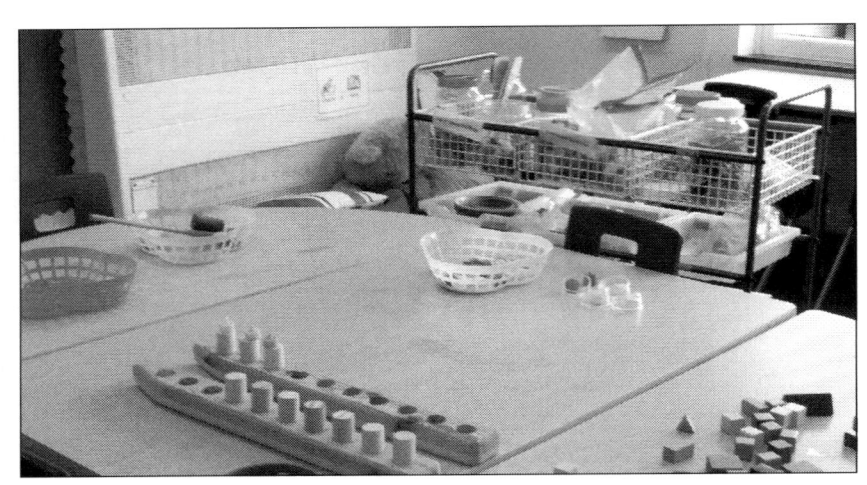

Generalisation of the learning to learn abilities

As the learning to learn sessions are based on the developmental needs of the children, it follows that similar activities should be available for the children during their 'free play' or 'explore time', whichever way it is described on the timetable. It has been noticed in many classrooms that the children spontaneously seek out the Waldon equipment to play with; they spend time posting, sorting, organising and scooping; children will always get absorbed in activities they understand.

It is possible to arrange a corner in the classroom with some of the equipment used in the structured sessions. Make available a small selection of objects for posting such as a box of blocks, bangles, a boat with pegs, a stand to thread the bangles onto, a muffin tray to arrange the objects in and a couple of tool-based activities. It is advisable to limit the amount of accessible materials at any one time, but to change them regularly; too much stuff can cause confusion and disorganisation!

The learning to learn skills and abilities are the child's essential tools to manage everyday tasks and it is clearly important to generalise these capacities into daily living. Take, for example, the understanding of expanding series: this transfers directly to stacking the mixing bowls according to size after washing up. Other tasks such as opening and closing jars or water bottles, using keys to open boxes, sorting the cutlery in the drawer, arranging the shoes in pairs etc., all require the application of the learning to learn capacities. Use everyday tasks to promote the child's understanding.

Further advice

Managing challenging behaviours during the session

It is important to keep the session going without disruptions, this helps the child to stay positively engaged. If the child uses challenging behaviours, try to figure out the reasons why and quickly make the necessary adjustments to the task. Most children will resort to such behaviours at some stage and it cannot always be prevented; the key is to respond in the right way.

- **No criticism or reprimands.** It is vital not to respond with reprimands or give attention to the behaviour; the child might like that reaction. Stay calm and quiet and carry on.
- **Hitting out.** It is best to ignore this behaviour and position yourself to avoid the hits if at all possible. One idea is to introduce a tool-use activity and to give full hand-over-hand support; this can stop the behaviour and will re-direct the child's attention to a new and less demanding task.
- **Throwing stuff.** If the child drops or throws something, leave it and keep going with the activity; tidy up when the child has left at the end of the session. Some children come to see tidying up as a posting game they enjoy, in which case, help each other to tidy the equipment at the end.
- **Freezing or going rigid.** If a child decides to 'freeze', don't attempt to force his hands. Instead, continue picking up and moving stuff around on your own, everything is carrying on as if he was taking part; let him sit and watch and more often than not, he will get involved again of his own accord.
- **Picking up handfuls of stuff is a labour-saving behaviour.** This behaviour can be discouraged by working quickly or using large blocks. It is also possible to flick the extra piece out of the child's hand with a finger; this makes the point of 'one at a time'. Continue to reinforce the correct behaviour without getting too rigid about it.
- **Getting up from the table.** The reason can be one of many: he is used to a short, task-based session and he always gets up when he has finished; he might also have sensory needs that can only be met by a quick walk. It is OK for the child to get up and move around a little, but he should be led back to the table, gently and without fuss, so he can carry on where he left off. The adult decides when the session is over.

Challenging behaviours can also be an indication that the child feels the activity is too demanding and is causing him anxiety. Reduce the demands by either lowering the level of complexity, or alternatively, introduce a different activity all together. It is essential to continue the session and to help the child to feel good again. This issue of challenging behaviours was also discussed in chapter 4.

Social interaction during the session

Despite the session being non-verbal there is still a close relationship between the adult and the child. Most children are sociable and they may seek to interact during the session, this is what they are used to. In my experience, it is OK to show the natural signs of feeling connected, but to avoid talking and any lengthy social interaction.

Share the feeling. The feeling of togetherness is usually present; there is enjoyment for both the child and the adult; after all, it is a joint experience. If the child looks at the adult to communicate this feeling, validate it by sharing eye-contact and a smile; this is entirely normal and natural. After that, carry on with the game.

Working in silence. It can be hard for some children to get used to the silence. The adult is not talking and she is not responding in a way they are used to or expect; this can cause them to behave in challenging ways. For these children, a gentle use of motherese can have a calming and settling effect. The key is to match the child's affect: use words like 'that's it', 'here we go', 'up it goes' etc. These are not instructions to the child, but simple 'background patter' which creates a soothing atmosphere. Once the child is settled, stop the patter and quietly carry on together. When they are familiar with the new way of working together, the issue generally subsides and they enjoy the quiet lesson.

The reasons for not giving praise

The child should not be given praise or verbal encouragement during the structured session. This is one of the most challenging aspects for adults to adhere to. They like to praise children and show them how pleased they are; it feels strange to them, not to give praise.

The reasons for this need some further explanation and we will see that well-meaning praise can create dependency and it can also be counter-productive to learning.

Let's look at it from the perspective of how young children learn. The child is playing on his own and every action he takes will always be based on his past experience: he will do what he already knows how. During his play, he has no 'correct' outcome in mind, but something unexpected will happen and he might notice and discover something new. If the adult praises the child for the final outcome, it implies the achievement of a goal, a goal which the child could not have been aware of. In short, the child will not understand why the adult is so pleased.

- Seeking approval from the adult is a learnt behaviour. Some children are conditioned to constantly look for affirmation, a sign that they are doing the 'right thing'; the adult's praise becomes a prompt on which they are dependent and they cannot carry on without it.
- Some children are highly sociable and they may become accustomed to receive effusive praise; their efforts can become linked to how pleased the adult appears to be.
- Praise is often given for specific outcomes; take for example building a tower with three bricks. The child has learnt to perform a set task which pleases the adult but it has added very little to his general understanding of brick-building; that will grow from exploring and creating variations.
- There is another critical point to remember: what happens when the praise is not forthcoming? The child will think: what did I do wrong, are they not pleased with me? He may feel he has been tested and failed, that there was an expectation he did not understand nor meet. This can make him anxious and ultimately affect his ability to engage and learn.

The pleasure in learning is derived from the effort of accomplishing the task itself.

Important note: Look after yourself

The method of sitting behind a child and guiding his hands to show him what to do, can potentially put strain on the adult's lower back; that should be avoided at all cost. The younger the child, the easier it will obviously be to work with him. Consider the comfort of the adult:

- The adult's chair must be high enough to guide the child's arms without leaning forward; a high stool may be a suitable option.
- When working with older children it is not comfortable to sit behind them. The alternative is to stand to the side and use a mixture of support: guiding the hand nearest to you, pointing or modelling.
- Sit next to each other and demonstrate what to do.

⑥ INITIAL ASSESSMENT OF THE LEARNING TO LEARN ABILITIES

This assessment will give an overview of a child's current level of functioning, identify his strengths and possible gaps in his understanding. This will be the starting point for future programmes of intervention.

- ▶ The initial assessment provides a thorough assessment of Levels 1 and 2 and touches upon the emerging capacities at Level 3.
- ▶ The assessment takes the same form as a regular structured teaching session. The attention is on the abilities the child demonstrates through the activities and how he responds to the situation.
- ▶ The assessment does not focus on which activities a child can complete, but on how he manages the tasks and what his behaviour tells us about his level of understanding.
- ▶ It is likely to take several working sessions to form a full picture of the child's learning to learn abilities and to assess his emotional maturity to manage new experiences.
- ▶ The observations can be recorded on the Initial assessment framework.

It is worth reiterating that the critical factor in the assessment is the facilitator's insights and her ability to analyse the child's responses to the new experiences: what does his behaviour tells us about his understanding and emotional well-being in the learning situation? The Initial assessment framework will capture sufficient information to provide a starting point for teaching. However, it is possible to look much deeper and create a narrative that describes the child's learning capacities, emotional responses and fragility during a working session; one such observation was written by Richard Brooks, *'Maria – A Description of an Asocial Lesson'*. This paper provides a valuable insight into the child's understanding and her emotional well-being during a lengthy working session with Geoffrey Waldon; it can be found on **www.waldonassociation.org.uk**

How to carry out an assessment

To carry out an assessment, treat the session like any other lesson. Follow the advice for adjusting the demands and moving up and down the levels on the developmental ladder, aiming to keep the child engaged throughout.

Approach to the tasks

The first consideration is the child's general approach to the tasks. This means looking for the following behaviours:

- Is he able to become and stay engaged for a substantial period of time? How long?
- Can he continue an activity unsupported once he understands the nature of it?
- Can he accept a change or variations to a familiar activity?
- Does he show signs of anxiety, if so, when/why does that happen?
- Does he use challenging behaviours to avoid a task?

Level 1: Fundamental movement abilities

Start with a 'picking up and putting in' activity such as placing wooden blocks into a basket or cubes into a jar; place all the equipment on the table. Begin by slowly doing the activity yourself, pick up and put the blocks in the basket, whilst carefully observing the child:

- Is he paying attention to what you are doing or is he looking elsewhere?
- Is he beginning to pick things up himself?

After a while, use a physical prompt, hand over hand, to get him involved. Once he is actively engaged, introduce new elements:

- Increase effort, use lots of objects. Does he pick up, post the objects and carry on in an effortful way?
- Create a strong rhythm, alternate picking up with the left and the right hand. Use a wider space, reaching out, up and across. Does he pick up the rhythm and is he familiar with the space around him?

- Use different objects and containers: note whether he spontaneously posts the pieces. Can he place them carefully such as filling a muffin tin? Are there any indications that he is beginning to choose what to pick up next?

Take careful note of his ability to manage these challenges as they are indicators of a well-integrated body and the beginnings of memory of order.

Level 1: Complementary use of hands and tool-use

The 'picking up and putting in' activities can be neatly changed into tool-use games: place a scoop in the child's hand and support him to pick up a brick and place it in the scoop, next transfer the brick to a saucepan. This task will show how well his two hands work together and his awareness of space.

- Use the scoop to rake in an object out of reach; can the child hold the tool, assess the problem and judge the distance?
- Jars with lids can be unscrewed and replaced; is the child able to use his hands together and can he hold tightly with one hand and rotate his wrist to remove the lid with the other?
- 'Banging and scraping' with two heavy spoons or sticks. Observe the child's reaction to this activity: Does he wonder about the noise or worry about it? Can he reach out and explore the wider space? Does he continue effortfully on his own?
- How confidently does the child hold the tools? Can he exert force when he is banging and can he continue a rhythmic pattern? Can he create movement patterns with a circular motion, side to side and up and down?

Level 2: Continuant capacity

The continuant capacity activities start with making a line of objects and then moving each element, one at a time, to a different place. For this activity, choose material that is stable and can be lined up and touching, such as wooden bricks, cylinders or plastic reels.

- Start a line of bricks along the edge of a board. Give the child one brick at a time. Can he continue the row?
- Can the child move a chain of pieces, one by one, from one place to another in order?
- The next step is to add another element to this chain; model for him how to place a cotton reel on top of each brick in order. Can the child find the next brick in the row and place the reel on it?
- Take this activity to the next level, whilst supporting the child to carry out the sequence:
    1. Remove the first reel and put this back in a tray.
    2. From another box, collect a wooden disc and place it on the now empty brick.
    3. Repeat these two actions all along the line of bricks, until every cotton reel is replaced by a disc.

  Can the child continue on his own? Does he make 'mistakes' along the way?
  Does he notice and can he change his mind?

The last example shows a two-step sequence with two different sets of objects, moving them consecutively from one place to another. If the child can continue on his own, his continuant capacity is developing.

Level 3: Emerging learning to learn capacities

It is helpful to include a couple of activities relating to the early learning to learn capacities, usually matching, sorting, seriation or piling. The full assessment of all the capacities for learning is included in chapter 9 alongside the activities.

Matching

This is the process of bringing together two objects which are very similar. Early matching is learning to make pairs, and is called Pairing. The first step is to teach the child the convention: when the adult shows an object in her palm, he has to locate the match and pass it to her. The game is described in detail under Matching in chapter 9.

Use a set of pairs of identical objects, items which are of little play interest to the child; this can be pairs of empty boxes, jam-jar lids, pieces of wood, two corks and so on. Spread four to six pairs out on the table; the adult picks up one and shows it in the hand; wait. Now point to the match and help the child to place it in the open hand. The pair is subsequently returned to the table, and the routine is repeated.

- Can the child attend to the object in the adult's hand?
- Can he resist the temptation to pick up the first object his eyes fall on?
- Can the child scan around and find the match?
- Can he hand over the object to the adult?
- Can he play this game in an ongoing way?

Sorting

This involves separating a collection of objects into several different sets, for example distinctly different collections such as coins, corks, clothes pegs and dice. Introduce the activity step by step in the following order:

1. Place one small bowl on the table, give the child a coin and indicate with a point that he should put the coin in the bowl; repeat with several coins.
2. Introduce the second set by placing another bowl on the table; present the child with one dice at a time, indicating this should go into the bowl.
3. Start afresh with both sets and present the objects at random. Now the child has to focus on each object before he decides where to deposit it.
4. Increase the number of sets and present the objects randomly.

In the process of playing this game, observe the child's capacity to separate the collections:

- Does the child check his piece against the objects in the tray before placing it?
- Using two collections, does the child tend to return to the tray where he has just placed an object? Can he focus on the new piece and does he remember both trays?
- Can the child continue to separate the two sets without help?
- If the child is given a tray with several sets mixed together, can he sort them into sets on his own?
- Does he pick out 'all the same' from the main stock?

Seriation

The early activities involve lining up some objects and this overlaps with the continuant capacity described above.

- ▶ Use the boat; prompt or show how to place the pegs in order into the holes. Can the child continue to the end?
- ▶ Make a chain of bricks, touching each other in a long row. Move the chain, brick by brick to a new location on the table; consider working from left to right, or right to left, or diagonally across the table. Can the child continue these patterns without support?
- ▶ Use two sets of objects. Start an alternating sequence like lid, cone, lid, cone. Can the child continue the pattern on his own?

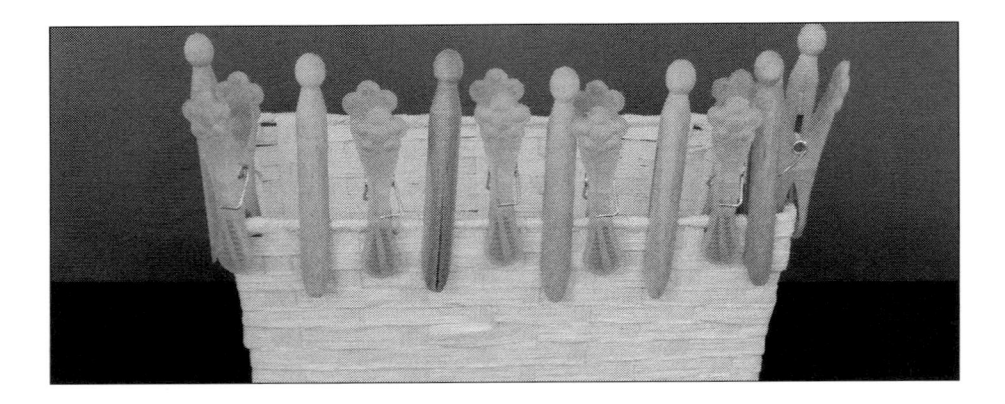

Piling

This is the first stage of brick-building and it is closely related to 'picking up and putting in', but instead of containing the objects they are made into a pile; this is not a stable structure and the pieces are likely to move or roll.

A pile can be started in a shallow dish to help define the space. Use a collection of non-uniform bits and pieces and deliver one at a time. The child's approach to making a random pile is an indicator of his awareness of spatial relationships and also his tolerance for unexpected events like the pegs falling off the pile.

- ▶ How does he place the pieces: randomly or deliberately?
- ▶ How does he react if they roll or move?
- ▶ Can he tolerate sharing the pile with the adult, who is adding her own pieces and thereby changing the pile?

Summary

All the information gathered during this assessment informs the starting point for the learning to learn sessions. This guidance for making observations and the structure of the assessment can be applied in future teaching sessions. Move onto section 3 for more information and ideas for activities at all levels.

Learning to learn: *Initial assessment framework*

Name:	Date:

Track: 0 = level not yet reached   / = emerging skill   X = competent skill

APPROACH TO TASK	Track	Observations
Is able to become and stay engaged		
Can continue activity unsupported		
Accepts change/variations in the activity		
Any signs of anxiety?		
Challenging behaviours impeding learning?		

LEVEL 1: FUNDAMENTAL MOVEMENT ABILITIES

Content	Abilities	Track	Observations
1. The appearance of physical effort	Reaches out		
	Grasps spontaneously		
	Will let go of objects		
	Places objects into tubs etc.		
	Is effortful		
	Continues unsupported		
2. Range and use of space	Crosses midline L/R/both		
	Reaches up/out/down/behind		
	Locates objects out of sight		
3. Picking up and putting in	Repeats action of picking up and putting in		
	Places an object in a defined space e.g. on a grid		
	Chooses between objects		
	Returns to the source of the objects		
4. Complementary use of hands and tool-use	Holds tools firmly in the hand		
	Bangs/scrapes rhythmically		
	Uses a scoop/spoon		
	Uses hands together, one as support to complete the task		
	Two-handed, twist lids on/off		
	Adapts the use of a tool to solve a problem		

LEVEL 2: CONTINUANT CAPACITY

Content	Abilities	Track	Observations
Engaging in continuant capacity	Makes a line of objects and moves them one by one to create a new line		
	Can continue a 'double line', one element with another on top, repeated in a line		
	Two step sequence: remove the element on top and replace it with a different object, all along the line		
	Continues a movement sequence of moving three sorts of objects, in a set order		

LEVEL 3: EMERGING LEARNING TO LEARN CAPACITIES

Content	Abilities	Track	Observations
Matching	Understands the game of making pairs by placing two identical objects together		
	Can look for an object to match the one he has been shown		
	Can ignore other items in the process of selecting the match		
Sorting	Separates into sets which are distinctly different		
	Sorts objects that are very similar but not identical		
	Sorts sets of cards with identical patterns using the sorting boards		
Seriation	Can move lines of objects one by one, from one place to another		
	Can continue a solid line of objects working in different directions		
	Can continue a chain of alternating objects		
Piling	Places objects randomly on a pile		
	Tolerates the objects moving or falling off		
	Places objects deliberately		

COMMENTS:

SECTION 3: PRACTICAL ACTIVITIES

Introduction

This section of the book gives step by step guidance to the activities at all levels and stages, arranged in line with the developmental framework.

There are three distinct developmental levels; this guidance describes the sub-skills that form part of the developmental ladder at each level and it is accompanied by a large number of practical activities to engage the child in learning.

Learning to learn

Chapter 7   Level 1: **Fundamental movement abilities**

Chapter 8   Level 2: **Continuant capacity**

Chapter 9   Level 3: **Learning to learn capacities**

Level 3: Stages of development	Stage 1: Early From around 24 months to 36 months	Stage 2: Active From 36 months, up to and around 48 months	Stage 3: Mature From 48 months, up to and around 60 months
Level 3: Learning to learn capacities	Matching		
	Sorting		
	Seriation		
	Drawing		
	Brick-building		

- ▶ In order to determine the child's approximate level of development, carry out the initial assessment described in chapter 6.
- ▶ The six **learning to learn capacities** which constitute level 3, are defined and illustrated in the relevant sections of chapter 9. The approximate stages of development can be identified and tracked using the learning to learn capacities developmental framework which can be found in appendix 3.
- ▶ Build the lesson in accordance with the advice on Implementing the learning to learn approach in chapter 5.
- ▶ Use the lesson planning format, listed in the appendix, to plan and review the sessions.

Children need to practise skills and abilities at all levels in every lesson.

> *Whenever you see this symbol, take a moment to reflect on the abilities the child is demonstrating at this point.*

7 LEVEL 1: FUNDAMENTAL MOVEMENT ABILITIES

Ideas for activities

At the early stages, the many skills and abilities are interlinked and develop simultaneously; in any given activity, several different movement abilities will be involved, skills. This is the reason why there are obvious similarities between all the early games.

Having established that the fundamental movement abilities are practised across the many activities, it is still essential to be clear why a particular game is chosen:

- ▶ What skills and abilities are being practised?
- ▶ Which movement patterns are encouraged?
- ▶ What is the level of complexity?

The focus is always on creating learning experiences. All the activities come with suggestions for equipment to use; however, this can always be substituted for something else which is more readily available. For example, use potatoes instead of bricks, bangles can replace the curtain rings, a muffin tray with corks can replace the wooden Waldon boat etc. The key is to adapt the available material to nurture the child's abilities; the equipment is only a means to an end.

The first section in this chapter covers movement abilities and physical effort. It encompasses the essential development of:

- ▶ Spontaneously reaching out.
- ▶ Grasping, picking up and letting go.
- ▶ Looking for the container and putting in.
- ▶ Keeping the momentum going on his own.

In choosing the material to use, make sure the equipment is safe and appropriate for the child's age and size. It must be a good match for the size of his hands so he can pick it up comfortably and he can reach the container to post it in. The objects must be weighty enough to give good sensory feedback; some plastic objects are too light which is why wooden bricks are often preferred. Look out for alternatives or make your own, such as small plastic containers filled with sand and sealed with tape. Avoid unstable items like balls that roll, as well as interesting toys because they can become a distraction in themselves.

Most of the activities are accompanied by ideas for variations; this is the crucial way to broaden the learning experiences for the child. Be creative when playing the games: the suggestions are not prescriptive, but instead adapt the equipment and the routines to provide countless new opportunities.

SECTION 3: PRACTICAL ACTIVITIES

1. Movement and physical effort

One set of objects and one container

EQUIPMENT: Bowl and bricks.

ACTIVITY: **Step 1.** Place the container on the table. Give the child one object after the other, every time placing it in a different location on the table. This requires the child to look around and focus on the next object to pick up. Do not worry about which hand he is using. Keep going with a large collection as this generates effort and momentum.

Step 2. Tip out the collection on the table. Guide the child to pick up the pieces one by one, first with one hand, then switch to the other hand to pick up lots more. Continue to pick up and fill the bowl.

Step 3. Empty out the bowl and start again. This time guide the child to pick up with alternate hands.

Lots of objects placed into one container

EQUIPMENT: Basket and one mixed collection of objects such as blocks, cones, lids, etc.

ACTIVITY: The child will experience the variation in weight and feel of objects in the process of putting them into a container.

Step 1. Scatter the collection all over the table and provide one central basket. Pick up the objects and put them into the basket, alternating the use of the left and the right hand.

Step 2. Move the basket so the child has to look around to locate it anew.

Step 3. Increase the speed and encourage a steady rhythm of picking up; this promotes focus and perseverance.

Lots of objects put into several containers

EQUIPMENT: Containers: baskets, bowls, trays, and objects: lids, rings, buttons, fir cones etc.

ACTIVITY: Place two different containers at opposite corners of the table and a central tray with lots of bits. Pick up one item at a time, alternate the hands for picking up. Switch between the two containers, one to the left and one to the right; everything will end up mixed together in the two containers.

VARIATIONS: **a.** Transfer everything from one container to the other, picking up one object at a time.

b. Introduce a third container. Spread the objects all over the table, pick up and post into one of the three pots at random. Do not attempt to sort; this ability will develop later.

Does the child continue to pick up and put in without help?

SECTION 3: PRACTICAL ACTIVITIES

2. Range and use of space

Posting into containers all around me

EQUIPMENT: Buckets and objects.

ACTIVITY: The aim is to increase the familiarity with the near body space and the ability to reach out accurately for the objects around.

Step 1. Start with one container and the objects spread around on the table. Pick up and put in, one at a time, alternating the use of the hands.

Step 2. Tip out the objects and start again. This time, keep moving the container round on the table, so each time a piece is posted, the container is in a different space.

Can the child coordinate his movements and reach out to a point away from his body?

VARIATIONS:

a. Move the container to the side of the child and place it on a chair.

b. Place the basket on a box on the table so the child has to reach up.

c. The facilitator holds the bowl and keeps moving around the child; he has to look around to find it, every time it is in a new position.

d. Place two or more containers in different positions. Use a large mixed collection of objects and post these, twisting and turning to reach out to the posting boxes.

Stick and ring game

EQUIPMENT: Stick, a little shorter than the child's arm, large curtain rings, basket.

ACTIVITY: This game develops the ability to focus on different points in space by locating the end of the stick. The child has to focus on this point and understand it is the end of the stick and then coordinate his movements to thread a ring on the stick.

Step 1. The child holds the stick in one hand and threads the ring onto it with the other.

Step 2. Reach out with the stick towards the basket, point it slightly downwards so the ring slides off and lands in the basket. If the ring misses the target, leave it where it fell and carry on. However, if it bothers the child that he has missed and he wants to try again, that's the way to continue.

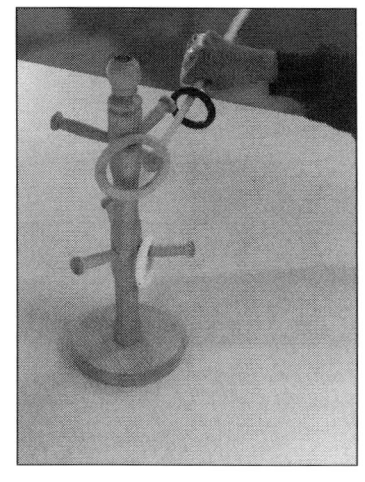

VARIATIONS:

a. The rings can be presented on a stand like a kitchen roll holder. The child removes one ring at a time and threads it onto the stick.

b. Practise holding the stick in either hand.

c. Change the position of the basket throughout the game to encourage scanning around.

d. Use a mug tree and thread a ring onto each of the branches.

Moving flowerpots with a stick

EQUIPMENT: Stick, a little shorter than the child's arm; stack of small flower pots, bucket.

ACTIVITY: Set up the game with the stack of small, plastic flower pots upside down on one side of the table, and the bucket positioned somewhere else out of reach.

Guide the child's hand to place one flower pot at the end of the stick, then reach out carefully to drop it into the bucket.

VARIATIONS: **a.** Place the bucket on a chair to the side of the child; it can only be reached with the stick.

b. Move the chair onto on the table, place the bucket on it; this will encourage stretching and reaching up.

c. Try the game with sticks of different lengths and weight.

Posting lolly sticks through a tube

EQUIPMENT: Cardboard tube, lolly sticks and a tray.

ACTIVITY: Hold the tube in one hand positioned over a tray; post the lolly sticks through the tube. The child must be aware of both the top and the bottom of the tube, where to drop the sticks and where will they come out.

VARIATIONS: **a.** Use tubes of different lengths and widths.

b. Build a two-step sequence: post a lolly stick through the tube into a flowerpot; empty the flowerpot into a second, larger container.

c. Use tubes of different lengths and shape, such as postal tubes which can be round, square or triangular as well as short or long.

Homemade posting boxes

EQUIPMENT: Make your own posting boxes out of empty tins with soft, plastic lids. Cut holes in the lids to fit a variety of small objects such as coins, straws, buttons.

ACTIVITY: Post the objects into the tin through the holes in the lid.

VARIATION: The posting box can be held in different positions, upright or lying on its side; the child has to adjust his movements to the new angle.

Crossing the midline, again and again

EQUIPMENT: Wooden boat as designed by Waldon with pegs; container.

As an alternative to the boat, use two muffin trays and 12 potatoes.

ACTIVITY: The primary focus is the ability to use the hands in the opposite body space, such as reaching across the midline to pick up or dispose of an object.

Step 1. Place the two halves of the boat on opposite sides of the table; move one peg at a time across, alternating the hands. The pegs can be moved in any order and the second boat is filled at random.

Step 2. Repeat, but change the position of the boats whilst maintaining the need to cross the midline.

Can the child reach across the midline? Is he equally comfortable with using his left and right hands in the opposite fields?

VARIATIONS: **a.** Place the full boat by the side of the child. He now has to turn his body to pick up a peg; arrange a box in the opposite corner of the table. Transfer the pegs, one by one, from the boat to the box.

b. Use the same set-up as above. This time the child holds a small jug in one hand: he picks up a peg, puts it in the jug, then reaches out and tips the peg into the box.

Building along with bricks and crossing the midline

EQUIPMENT: Two containers with wooden bricks; wooden boat.

ACTIVITY: Remove the pegs and position the two boats in extension of each other, upside down. The boats serve to define the space where the bricks should be lined up. Place the two containers with bricks on either side of the table.

Step 1. Reach across with the left hand to pick up a brick from the right-hand container; place this brick alongside the boat; repeat with the right hand, reaching across to the container in the corner opposite. Continue to create a long line of bricks alongside the boats.

Step 2. Reverse the exercise and dismantle the line, brick by brick. Post the bricks back into the containers, keeping the routine of using alternate hands to reach for the basket on the opposite side.

VARIATIONS: **a.** After creating the first line of bricks, continue by adding a second layer like building a wall.

b. Pick up two bricks, one in each hand. Place one on top of the other to create lots of towers of two bricks. Reverse this activity to dismantle the towers; every time cross over the midline and post into the containers on the opposite sides.

SECTION 3: PRACTICAL ACTIVITIES

3. Picking up and putting in

There are a number of skills to master when developing the abilities for 'picking up and putting in'. The child must be able to:

- ▶ Pick up and let go of the object in order to drop it into a container.
- ▶ Alternate attention between several containers.
- ▶ Place an object with care in a clearly defined space.

The first two skills overlap with the 'movement and effortful activities' and 'range and use of space' which were covered above. The third area, the skill of placing an object in a defined space, is a progression from dropping everything into an open container.

This new step requires the understanding of what constitutes a space: the child has to focus his attention on one particular point and he must coordinate his movements to reach and place the object in that space. This ability to focus and position an object with care should be practised through structured exercises when the child is ready.

Move the pegs from one boat to the other

EQUIPMENT: Wooden boat with pegs.

ACTIVITY: The aim is to develop the understanding that an object can be placed in a defined space.

Step 1. Place one empty boat on the table and give the child one peg at a time to fit into the boat. The pegs can be placed in any order. Continue until the boat is full.

Step 2. Present the second half of the boat. Guide the child's hands to transfer one peg at a time, starting with the first one in the boat; this is placed in the first hole on the second boat. Continue with support to ensure the pegs are placed in order.

Step 3. Gradually reduce the support to allow the child to make his own decision. If necessary, step in and guide the child to ensure he continues to fill up the boat in the set order.

VARIATION: Repeat the sequence of moving the pegs: this time work from right to left. Support can be given by pointing to the next hole along.

Does the child notice and understand how to place a piece in a specific spot?

Fill up the muffin tray, one in every hole

EQUIPMENT: Two muffin trays and objects which fit into the holes, such as small blocks or fir cones.

ACTIVITY: **Step 1.** Place one muffin tray on the table; present one block at a time to be placed in a hole. Continue until every hole is filled.

Step 2. Introduce another tray and move the blocks singly, step by step.

VARIATION: Use smaller objects where two could fit into the holes but shouldn't! Encourage the child to look for the empty spaces in the tray; allow only one piece in each hole.

Arrange the blocks in order on the H-board

EQUIPMENT: H-board, large blocks which fit within the spaces on the board.

ACTIVITY: The aim is to notice and understand what defines a space, and secondly to be able to place a block with precision in that spot.

With the H-board on the table, give the child one block at a time and point to a space on the board. Guide him to place the block to the space, holding his hand to ensure it is positioned accurately; the block must not be set down across two spaces. Continue to fill the whole H-board.

VARIATIONS: **a.** Practise placing the blocks in order, one in each space from left to right or right to left. Support with hand over hand or by pointing as necessary.

b. Fill the top row on the H-board in sequence. Then move each block to the space below, also working in order.

SECTION 3: PRACTICAL ACTIVITIES

Sorting boards have defined spaces

EQUIPMENT: Two sorting boards (3x3 grids).

Collections of small pieces that fit into the spaces on the boards e.g. bottle tops, rings, buttons, lids etc.

ACTIVITY: **Step 1.** Start with one sorting board and present the child with one piece at a time. These can be placed at random on the sorting board but they must sit clearly within a space.

Step 2. Once the grid is completed, transfer the pieces one by one, to a second sorting board.

VARIATIONS: **a.** Place one block in each space on the sorting board. Extend the activity by adding a smaller brick on top of every block.

b. Prompt the child to fill one column at a time, working systematically top to bottom along the grid.

c. Give the child a trayful of pieces; he completes the boards without support.

Too many objects to fit into the available spaces! What does the child do: pile them all on the board or does he know when to stop?

Pots and saucers go together, all in a row

EQUIPMENT: Set of plastic flowerpots and saucers; fir cones.

ACTIVITY: The aim is to develop an understanding of one-to-one correspondence: each saucer needs a pot, one cone in every pot. Once the line of objects has been created, it can be dismantled by moving one piece at a time; this helps with switching attention from one to the other, and keeping a rhythm going.

Step 1. Place the stack of flower pots at one side of the table and the pile of saucers on the opposite side. Pick up one of each and place the flower pot on the saucer; arrange them all in a row.

Step 2. Once the row is complete, introduce the box of fir cones. Place one cone into every flowerpot, work in order along the row.

VARIATION: Use a muffin tray and two different sets of small objects. Start with the first set and place one in every hole; repeat with the second set, adding another piece to every hole.

4. Complementary use of hands and tool use

When the child can use both hands together to perform a task, he is developing the ability referred to as the *complementary use of hands*. For the new-born baby, the two arms function as separate parts and the hands are simple extensions of his arms. Before long, the baby becomes very aware of his hands and he explores them in his mouth and in front of his face. The baby has a grasp reflex from birth, but when he is three to four months old, he will actively try to grasp a toy with both hands. This develops into the amazing ability to manipulate and coordinate the movements of the hands, with the left and right hand working together.

The use of tools grows out of the early behaviour of banging and scraping; this starts around the time when the baby can sit up and he can keep a firm grip on a toy. At this stage the baby is waving his arms around and he is not focused on the toy in his hand. But soon he notices what happens when he accidentally strikes another surface with the toy – something made a noise! The baby becomes aware that the object in his hand is an extension of his body: that's why the noise happened. This leads to the next phase when the baby starts to bang and scrape with intent. He has discovered the movements that makes a noise, he liked it and he can do it again!

This is the beginning of tool-use, the discovery that objects can be applied to create new possibilities. Many objects can become tools, they can be adapted for a new purpose. Take, for example, a spoon, it can be used in many ways: it is good for banging, it can also make marks in the yogurt on the plate and it can even put food in the mouth. The baby is learning about how to make a noise, about making marks as well as incidentally, eating.

The interest in mark-making develops at this time. Given the opportunity, the baby explores how to make marks, he takes a real interest in the effect of the movements of his arm and the tool: this can be a stick on the ground or a crayon on paper. He looks at the patterns he creates, the lines and scribbles. This particular experience is the beginnings of drawing which is one of the learning to learn capacities.

Many seemingly simple activities such as scooping sand into a bucket relies on a complex set of underlying and unspecialised movement skills:

- Holding the scoop.
- Digging down.
- Lifting it up and keeping it level.
- Grasping and steadying the bucket with the other hand.
- Reaching to empty the sand out etc.

It is essential to provide the child with many and diverse opportunities to develop the strength and dexterity in both hands as well as the underlying movement abilities necessary for the two hands to complete the tasks together. The principle is to provide the widest possible range of learning experiences, always incorporating extensive variations. Similar activities are also described in the section on the development of drawing in chapter 9.

Rhythmic banging

EQUIPMENT: Weighty banging toys such as wooden hammers, rods made from a broomstick handle or large spoons.

ACTIVITY: **Step 1.** Guide the child in a pattern of effortful, rhythmic banging on the table:

- Large up and down movements.
- Vary the speed between slow and fast banging.
- Small movements mixed with large movements.

Step 2. Explore the different feel and sounds around the table when banging:

- On the table top.
- On the table legs.
- Bang with the left hand whilst the right is resting, then reverse.
- Bang with both hammers together in the same pattern.
- Create simple repeating patterns - bang, bang, pause; bang, bang, pause!

VARIATION: Introduce a saucepan to create new sounds; alternate banging on the table and on the saucepan. Pick up the saucepan and 'stir' it with the stick, that makes a new noise.

Scraping movements with sticks

EQUIPMENT: Weighty banging toys such as two rods, spoons or wooden hammers.

ACTIVITY: The purpose of this exercise is to feel the large movements and the great variety of patterns. The activity follows on naturally from banging and scraping above.

Support the child by either helping him to hold the rods and move them together, or you both hold on without touching but the adult guides the movements.

Step 1. Hold a rod in each hand, make 'scraping' movements on the table in various patterns with both hands together:

- Large circular movements on the table top.
- Left to right and right to left.

- Sweeping movements diagonally across the table.
- Move slowly and deliberately, change the speed.

Step 2. Introduce different patterns to the ones suggested above, and practise these, first with the left hand, then the right, then both hands together.

VARIATION: Tape a piece of paper to the table. Hold a chunky crayon in each hand and repeat the same movement patterns as above. The child will have a chance to observe the outcome of a movement.

The movements can be practised without holding onto anything; the child will feel the space, rhythm and patterns.

Lots of banging and scraping

EQUIPMENT: Weighty banging toys as mentioned above.

ACTIVITY: The purpose is to combine the banging and scraping movement patterns in a single, prolonged exercise. Explore the variety of movement patterns from the two previous activities, mixing the two together and creating variations and repeats. Observe the child carefully and be aware of how he feels during the activity: is he effortful and does he continue without support? Some children need time and practice before they can lose themselves in the banging and scraping exercises.

Use a spoon to transfer the blocks

EQUIPMENT: Large spoon, a collection of wooden blocks and a container.

ACTIVITY: **Step 1.** Spread the blocks on the table. Hold a large spoon in one hand and support the child to pick up one block and place it in the spoon; reach out with the spoon and transfer the block to the container.

Step 2. Continue this routine whilst moving the container around on the table; this means practising a different movement with every block.

Step 3. Swap hands and repeat the game.

VARIATIONS: **a.** Use a mixed collection to pick up. Every object will have a different weight and feel.

b. Change the spoon: it can be deep or shallow, have a short or a long handle, feel light or heavy to hold.

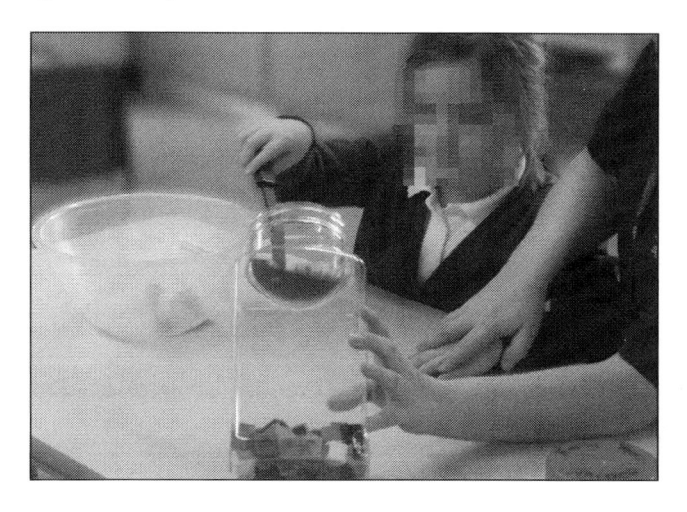

SECTION 3: PRACTICAL ACTIVITIES

Scooping

EQUIPMENT: Sand-play scoop and a jug.
Fir cones or other small objects in a bowl.

ACTIVITY: Use the scoop to transfer the fir cones from the bowl to the jug. It is important to support the child's hands to carry out the two different functions, one to steady the bowl and the other to use the scoop.

VARIATIONS:
a. Change over and practise the same skills with the opposite hands.

b. Use different implements as scoops: a wooden spoon with a longer handle, or a small spoon which only holds one cone at a time.

c. Choose containers of different shapes and height to create new experiences; vary their position on the table.

Dustpan and brush

EQUIPMENT: Dustpan and brush, mixed collection of objects, box.

ACTIVITY: Spread the small objects on the table top. With the dustpan and brush, make large sweeping movements to brush the objects into the dustpan; transfer them to the box. The aim is to create familiarity with the range of movements, not to teach tidying up!

VARIATIONS:
a. Swap hands and practise the movements with both hands.

b. Hold the dustpan below the table edge and sweep the fir cones into it; empty the dustpan into a bowl after each sweeping movement.

c. The same sweeping action can be achieved with a stick in one hand and a scoop in the other.

d. Use a collection of heavy pieces to sweep up.

Picking up with a spoon and a fork

EQUIPMENT: Spoon and fork, dried conkers, jug.

ACTIVITY: **Step 1.** Place a shallow tray of conkers on the table. Give the child a fork and a spoon and guide him to use the two together. Once the conker is on the spoon, tip it into the jug.

Step 2. Swap the spoon and fork to the other hand and practise the activity again.

VARIATIONS:
a. Change the size and location of the container.

b. Practise with various small objects; these can be presented in a tray, a bowl or on a non-slip mat.

c. Try out different spoons and forks, the handle and weight can vary a lot.

SECTION 3: PRACTICAL ACTIVITIES

Unscrewing lids from jars

EQUIPMENT: Jars with screw-top lids; in preparation, put a cork inside every jar.

ACTIVITY: The focus here is on the experience of using the two hands together, one hand holding the jar steady and the second hand rotating the wrist to remove the lid. This activity has been broken down into several steps but it can be simplified and adapted to suit the child. It is the quality of the movements that is important.

- Present one closed jar at a time.
- Remove the lid and place this in a saucer.
- Tip the cork out into the other hand and post it into a box.
- Replace the lid on the jar.
- Place the jar in a tray.

VARIATION: When the child can confidently complete all the steps, add the extra step of replacing the cork with a straw before the lid is screwed back on.

Look for sturdy bottles with substantial lids; the large lids will enable a good grip and rotation of the wrist.

Threading large rings onto a piece of rope

EQUIPMENT: Piece of rope, curtain rings or bangles, kitchen roll stand.

ACTIVITY: Secure the end of the rope with a large ring, tape the other end to prevent the rope from fraying.

Step 1. Give the child the piece of rope, guide him to find the end. Present one ring at a time; thread the ring onto the rope, pulling it right to the end.

Step 2. Remove one ring at a time and place it on the stand.

VARIATIONS: **a.** Present the rings on the stand; the child has to remove one at a time.

b. Use rings of different sizes and materials.

c. In preparation for the activity, thread the rings onto the rope and tie a single knot around each ring. Now the child has to untie the knot in order to remove the rings.

Raking in

EQUIPMENT: Small toy rake, bricks and a box.

ACTIVITY: Spread the bricks on the table, well out of the child's reach. Introduce the small toy rake, watch the child: does he spontaneously use the rake to get hold of the bricks? If necessary, demonstrate the action or guide the child to rake in the bricks. When they are within reach, pick them up and post them in the box.

VARIATIONS: **a.** Use a different implement to 'rake in' with, such as a wooden spoon or a cardboard tube.

b. As each brick is retrieved, build a wall instead of putting them in the box.

Open with a lever

EQUIPMENT: Tins with press-down metal lids; metal spoon.

ACTIVITY: In preparation, put a small object inside each tin and fix the lid back on.

Give the child a tin and a spoon. Rattle the tin and observe his response: does he know what to do? Pick at the lid unsuccessfully, then show him how the spoon can be used as a lever, without opening the tin. Pass the spoon to the child and support him to open the tin. Once it is open, remove the object inside and press the lid back on.

VARIATION: In preparation, place a piece from a puzzle in each tin; as the pieces are removed, the puzzle is assembled.

Picking up with tongs

EQUIPMENT: Choice of tongs, e.g. BBQ tongs, sugar tongs.

Collection of small objects that fit the size of the tongs such as Unifix cubes, small fir cones; containers.

ACTIVITY: **Step 1.** Present the small fir cones in a shallow tray. Hold the tongs in one hand whilst the other is used to steady the tray. Transfer the fir cones into the bowl, one by one, with the tongs.

Step 2. Swap hands and transfer the fir cones back into the tray.

VARIATIONS: **a.** Use containers of different heights and shapes, move them around on the table.

b. Try a variety of small items to pick up with the tongs; smooth objects need a firm grip; small furry craft balls will be easier to catch and hold.

Explore many different opening mechanisms

EQUIPMENT: Gather a mixed selection of containers with different lids and opening mechanisms – screw lids, plastic lids that flip off, money box with a key, tins with lids to lever off, small string bags, zip plastic wallets etc.

ACTIVITY: In preparation, place an object inside each container.

Present the child with one container at a time to open and remove the object inside. When giving the child support, emphasise the correct movements of both hands together, exaggerate the hold and twist motion. The longer it takes the child to open a box, the more he learns.

VARIATIONS: **a.** Replace the object which has been removed, before closing the container again.

b. Create containers with multiple layers: for example, put a puzzle piece in a small string bag into a zip-wallet inside a plastic tub with a lid. This will target many skills and the need for perseverance.

8 LEVEL 2:
CONTINUANT CAPACITY

This is the ability to *remember and to choose between objects and to move them from place to place in sequence and to keep going*. As mentioned previously, this is quite literally the carrier phase for learning to learn, and it is vital for developing an understanding of the world.

The capacity emerges from 'picking up and putting in', leading to the growing understanding of movement sequences which are deliberate and planned. The child is choosing what to pick up and where to put it, and he decides how to arrange the play pieces in some kind of order. He continues this activity by moving the toys, piece by piece, around the room; the game is ongoing and never ends!

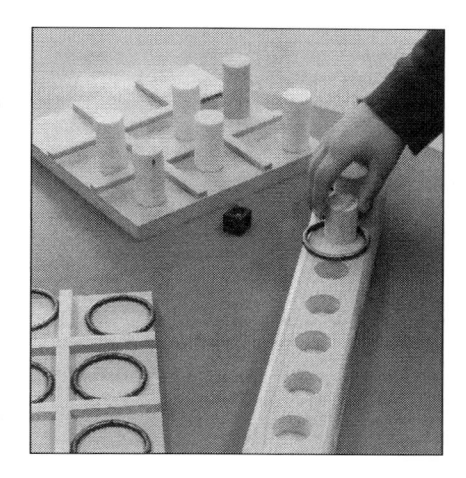

Development of the continuant capacity

The steps in the teaching process can be described in terms of three stages, and the activities that follow are organised accordingly:

Stage 1. Pointing and scanning along

These activities help to practise the child's ability to look along his arm to the pointing finger at the end. He has to follow this point with his eyes along a row of objects, be it the pegs in the boat or a line of yogurt pots with a lolly stick in each. The aim is to identify the end of the row and to understand this is the next space to be filled.

Stage 2. Moving two collections from place to place in order

The child must be able to keep in mind two different collections and switch his attention between them. This involves the ability to move an object from one of the sets to a different place, then to pick up a piece from the second collection and position that somewhere new; the important next step is to return to the first set where the movement sequence started and do it all again. He has to remember 'First I take the peg out and put it in the box; then I find the spatula and put it in hole; now I go back for another peg...', many times over.

Stage 3. Moving three or more collections around in a given order

This is an extension of the ability described above, but it involves moving around three or more different groups of objects; this requires the ability to remember complex movement sequences, to switch attention between the objects, and to remember pieces that may be out of sight.

Teaching technique

General set-up

These activities are extensions of the earlier movement activities and follow naturally on from placing and lining up during the structured session. The aim is for the child to continue the activity independently and to work at his own pace.

- The facilitator devises the movement sequences, selecting the objects and the containers for the activity.
- The child should be prompted through the first steps to help him notice the sequence. Reduce the help when he begins to anticipate the next action, but be ready to step in and help again as necessary; the movement pattern should be continued as it was intended from the start.
- Independence comes when the child can take over and carry on by himself.
- The first game should be a simple two-step sequence, to which more steps can be added to increase the level of complexity.
- The level of support should be adjusted to keep the child focused and can change several times throughout one exercise:
    1. Physical prompt, which is guidance with hand over hand.
    2. Modelling, i.e. showing the child what to do by moving the pieces for him.
    3. Pointing, to show the next step.

Role of the facilitator

The crucial role of the facilitator is to give the child new and varied experiences and to facilitate independence in the learning activities. The adult must be tuned in to how well the child is managing the task: is he enjoying it, is it still within his level or is he showing signs of anxiety?

- If a child pauses and appears to feel muddled, observe carefully; wait and give him time to problem-solve by himself. When the child is thinking, he is learning.
- Step in sensitively with a point if the child appears confused or anxious.
- Should it become clear that the activity is too difficult, let the child finish it at his own level without trying to correct him; this prevents any sense of failure.
- Adjust the next game to be well within his level or change the focus completely to another skill area altogether; this can keep him engaged in the session.

Equipment

Pieces to move around

Use collections of 'bits and bobs' that fit into the containers and the spaces on the H-board e.g. corks, pegs, blocks, bobbins, fir cones, lids etc.

Containers

Use a stack of plastic flower pots, yogurt pots, plastic saucers, small bottles, a muffin tray, empty chocolate box as well as the H-board and the wooden boat.

ACTIVITIES

STAGE 1
Pointing and scanning along

These activities develop the child's ability to follow his pointing finger with his eyes, combined with the ability to coordinate the movements to place an object at the finger point; the two hands meet at this point which is the next space along the line.

Follow the pointing finger with the eyes

EQUIPMENT: H-board and a collection of identical cubes.

ACTIVITY: The aim is for the child to understand where to place the cube: the space he is pointing to at the end of the row.

These instructions are very detailed and they can be simplified and adjusted in response to the child's ability to continue the movement sequence on his own; there is no need to follow them rigidly.

Step 1. Turn the H-board upside down and use the edge to build along. Start a row with three or four cubes.

Step 2. Help the child to pick up a cube in one hand; shape his other hand into a point with support. Move the pointing finger along the row of cubes, one by one, until he reaches the empty space at the end of the row. Rest the pointing finger here and place the cube next in the row.

Step 3. Pick up another cube and repeat as above; continue and create a long row of cubes.

VARIATIONS: **a.** Repeat the pointing and placing game, this time swapping the hands over to be the 'pointer' and the 'picker-upper'.

b. Build a row in the opposite direction, working from right to left.

It takes practice to understand how to point along a row and find the end. Work slowly through many variations of this activity.

Track the pointing finger in different directions

EQUIPMENT: H-board and a mixture of small objects in a basket.

ACTIVITY: The aim is for the child to point to the next space on the board and place an object there.

Step 1. Support the child to point to the first space on the H-board and place a small item in the space with his other hand.

Step 2. Move the pointing finger along to the next gap and fill it.

Step 3. Maintain support for pointing, but reduce the prompt for placing. When the child moves his pointing finger along to the next space, it is time to withdraw and allow him to continue on his own.

VARIATIONS: **a.** Work along the H-board from left to right in the top section, turn the corner and continue back along the bottom section; this means moving in the opposite direction.

b. Repeat the exercise with different objects.

c. Position the H-board to work diagonally; start near the body, point and place further and further away; reverse the direction.

Pointing and lining up

EQUIPMENT: Set of blocks.

ACTIVITY: It is harder to work in an open space than it is to line up along the edge of a box or on the H-board with the marked divisions. The aim is to develop the understanding that a line of objects can be arranged in an open space.

Step 1. Work on the open table, start a chain with three or four blocks.

Step 2. Demonstrate pointing to each piece along the chain, then rest at the space at the end; add another block.

Step 3. Guide the child to point all along and rest at the end; place a block there. Continue to create a long chain, 'point to the next space along, place the block'.

VARIATIONS: **a.** Play the game with objects that have small variations in form such as stones or fir cones; this will make the chain slightly irregular.

b. Work the chain in different directions e.g. starting in the corner of the table and working diagonally across.

STAGE 2
Moving two collections from place to place in order

These activities require the child to carry out two movement sequences and switch his attention between two collections and two locations. He can practise this with a routine such as 'First I get the bottle from the box, then I find a clothes-peg and put it in; now the box goes in the basket ...', many times over.

The sequences are described in detail and they sound very complex when they are written down. Try to follow the descriptions and practise the sequence of moves on your own first; you will experience the activities in the same way as the child. Play around with finding new variations, keeping careful count of the steps involved.

Games with the wooden boat

EQUIPMENT: The wooden boat with pegs, box of spatulas and corks. Tray.

SEQUENCE: To prepare the sequence, place the boat with the wooden pegs on the table, an empty tray and a box with spatulas.

Step 1. Demonstrate the sequence starting by removing a peg from the boat and placing it in the tray; next, find a spatula and place it in the empty hole.

Step 2. Repeat the steps above; help the child to complete every action to ensure he gets it right. Step back and let the child take over when he is ready.

Please note, it is important to move one piece at a time; the child might be tempted to collect up all the pegs in one go, and then fill the boat with spatulas. That approach greatly reduces the number of decisions the child has to make and should be discouraged.

VARIATIONS: **a.** Start with the boat filled with spatulas. This time, remove a spatula, put it in a bottle; next place a cork in the empty hole where the spatula was. Repeat.

b. Try different collections of objects which will fit into the boat.

c. Work from right to left and left to right.

SECTION 3: PRACTICAL ACTIVITIES

Games with wooden pegs and curtain rings

EQUIPMENT: The boat with wooden pegs, curtain rings on a stand and small cubes.

SEQUENCE: Set-up: empty the boat and present the wooden pegs in a tray and the curtain rings on a stand. Demonstrate the first steps, then guide the child to complete the movement sequence.

Step 1. Place one wooden peg in the boat, fit a ring over it. Carry on and fill up the boat in this fashion: peg + ring.

Step 2. Remove the first ring and return it to the stand; place a cube on the peg. Continue all along: one ring off, one cube on top.

VARIATIONS: **a.** When removing the rings, line them up on the H-board instead of placing them back on the stand.

b. Increase the complexity of the game above by introducing another step:

- Remove the cube, put it in a box.
- Move the peg from the boat and place it inside a curtain ring on the H-board.

Bricks, cotton reels and buttons

EQUIPMENT: Bricks, cotton reels and buttons.

SEQUENCE: Prepare the activity: place the box of bricks on a chair by the child's side. He now has to turn his body to pick them up; position the tray of cotton reels on the table. Follow the process of first demonstrating the sequence, then guiding the child to continue the activity and allowing him to carry on unsupported.

Step 1. Pick up a brick, line it up against the edge of the table; place a cotton reel on top. Continue to make a long chain.

Step 2. Start at either end of the chain; remove the cotton reel and put a button in its place.

VARIATIONS: **a.** Change the materials used to place on the bricks.

b. Arrange the bricks with a small gap in between so they are no longer touching each other. Add a piece on top of each brick.

c. Keep the containers at either side of the child's chair so they are no longer in view. Dismantle the double chain, one piece at a time; the child has to turn and look for the containers by his side.

Can the child continue the alternating movement sequence without help?

Flowerpot game

EQUIPMENT: Stack of plastic flower pots, box of blocks and fir cones.

ACTIVITY: Set-up: Place a stack of flowerpots, upside down on the table; box of blocks.

Step 1. Take one flowerpot and place a block inside.

Step 2. Repeat until all the flowerpots are lined up with a block inside.

Step 3. Introduce the fir cones; these will now replace the blocks inside the flower pots, one by one. This is the routine:

- Empty the block out of the flowerpot into the open hand.
- Drop the block into a bowl.
- Find a fir cone to place into the flowerpot.
- Repeat all the steps with every pot.

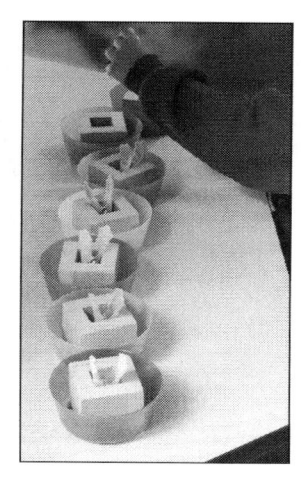

VARIATION: Start with a stack of empty flowerpots, a box of lids and a tray with pegs:

- Pick up a lid and put it in the flowerpot.
- Add a peg to the same pot; there are now two different things in the pot one of which may be hidden under the other.
- Remove the lid from the flowerpot and replace it with a button.
- Make this exchange for all the pots, leaving the pegs in place.

Spice jars and pegs

EQUIPMENT: Spice jars with lids, H-board, corks and small cubes.

ACTIVITY: In preparation, place the H-board on the table, a collection of empty spice jars and a tray with corks.

Step 1. Pick up a jar and put a cork inside; place the jar in the first space on the H-board, pointed out by the adult.

Step 2. Repeat this sequence until all the jars are on the H-board with a cork inside. The H-board does not need to be filled completely.

Step 3. Work through the whole series again, but this time tip out the cork, put it in a tray; replace it with a cube and return the jar to its place on the board.

VARIATION: Screw a lid on all the jars; this adds the extra movements of opening and closing, using the hands together.

STAGE 3
Moving three or more collections around in a given order

The activities above can easily be extended from two-step sequences to games with three or more steps; this obviously increases the level of complexity considerably. At this level, the child is expected to work more or less independently after the initial demonstration and guidance through the steps.

The complex movement sequences are challenging; the child might start OK, but then he leaves out one element. He may later notice this and incorporate it back into the pattern; he may also continue without it or create his own variation. These are all essential learning experiences and great sensitivity is needed to know when to let the child continue his pattern and when to step in and redirect him.

Some children get confused when they play several variations of the sequencing games with the same selection of toys; it is helpful to change the materials along the way whilst maintaining the same level of difficulty.

Sequence with a muffin tray

EQUIPMENT: Muffin tray, bricks, bottle tops and curtain rings on a stand.

ACTIVITY: The complexity of this game builds up gradually with each step. It is advisable to have a go without the child; this ensures the adult has a clear picture in mind of the movement sequence.

Step 1. Place a brick in each hole of the muffin tray; emphasise the order of working from left to right and completing one row after the other.

Step 2. Place a bottle top on each brick, working in the same order.

Step 3. Remove the bottle top, lift the brick up and place a ring underneath it; return the bottle top. There is now a hidden element to remember.

Step 4. Remove the bottle top and place it in a box, remove the ring from underneath the brick; the brick is returned to the original place in the tray.

VARIATIONS: **a.** Start by placing a small disc in every hole, add the brick on top. Remove one disc at a time from underneath the brick, followed by placing a shell on top of the brick.

b. Place the trays with the small items out of view, for example on a chair next to the child; he has to remember where to find the pieces.

Saucers, bits and pieces!

EQUIPMENT: Plastic saucers, shells, cubes and clothes pegs.

ACTIVITY: Place a stack of saucers on the table, a tray of cubes and another one with shells.

Step 1. Take a saucer and put in both a shell and a cube; arrange the saucers in a long line on the table.

Step 2. Go back to the beginning and one by one, remove the cube and fix a clothes peg on the edge of the saucer; continue all along, switching attention between the different elements, cubes, shells and clothes pegs.

VARIATION: Change the pattern above: place a ring on the peg and remove the shell from the saucer.

Complex sequence with boat

EQUIPMENT: Boat, small spatulas and corks.

ACTIVITY: Arrange the two halves of the boat on the table, one with a spatula in each hole, the other with the pegs in place; tray of corks and an empty tub.

There are three steps to complete in the set order:

Step 1. Post the first spatula into the tub.

Step 2. Transfer the first peg into the now vacant hole.

Step 3. Place a cork in the hole vacated by the peg.

Step 4. Continue this sequence, move one item at a time in the set order.

The ability to monitor and have a change of mind, is significant. Work slowly and allow plenty of thinking time.

VARIATIONS: Similar sequences can be developed with the boat, a muffin tray or the H-board, keeping in mind the movement of three different elements, e.g.

> ▶ Move a peg from the boat to the H-board; put a cube on top and a cork in the vacant hole on the boat.

> ▶ Remove the cork from the boat; put the cube in the hole and a ring around the peg on the H-board.

SECTION 3: PRACTICAL ACTIVITIES

9 LEVEL 3
LEARNING TO LEARN CAPACITIES & ACTIVITIES

The ***learning to learn capacities*** are the universal, mental systems for organising our understanding of the world. These are the essential tools we need to make sense of our experiences and learn; they are used in all new learning situations throughout life.

At the previous level 2, we saw the development of the continuant capacity, which grows out of the child's ability to handle objects and move them around in a planned and organised fashion. In so doing he begins to notice their unique properties and attributes and these new experiences get processed utilising the learning to learn capacities, the cognitive abilities to analyse and organise information; these experiences accumulate and become our general understanding. Geoffrey Waldon used the term mental learning to learn tools to describe these capacities.

The six learning to learn capacities are distinct but closely linked and interconnected and they develop simultaneously. The six capacities are:

- Matching
- Sorting
- Seriation
- Drawing
- Brick-building
- Coding

The learning to learn capacities develop gradually with many small steps along the way. There are three significant milestones and these are used to define and describe three stages to create a developmental framework; the stages cover the chronological age span from around 24 months to 60 months.

Stage 1: Early stage, the abilities acquired between 24 and 36 months.

Stage 2: Active stage, from 36 months up to and around 48 months.

Stage 3: Mature stage, from 48 months to 60 months and beyond.

In the sections which follow, there is one chapter dedicated to each learning to learn capacity, where the developmental milestones are described in detail. This three-stage framework will help to focus on the developmental age of the child and support the planning of activities to help him progress.

Each structured session with a child should incorporate activities relating to one or maybe two learning to learn capacities; there is not time to address all areas of development in one lesson. However, over time, these experiences will accumulate to broaden and deepen his learning to learn capacities, and when he encounters a new situation in everyday life, he will naturally and unconsciously use all his learning to learn capacities to process the experiences. Take, for example, a child who is attempting to copy a pattern: in the process he will be looking for similarities and differences, which are the mental tools of sorting and matching; he will look for repeating patterns which is using his seriation ability; he will look for how the elements are positioned next to each other, which is 2-D and 3-D praxis. All his learning to learn capacities have been engaged.

The table below shows the parallel and simultaneous development of the learning to learn capacities. The name given to each stage describes the significant abilities which are new at that stage. They are also an aide-mémoire which can help with structuring the teaching sessions.

Always bear in mind that the child's abilities will grow at different rates across the learning to learn capacities; they develop in parallel but also feed into each other. It is beneficial to include a range of experiences at different levels during the sessions. This will help the child to move up the developmental ladder.

Coding is not included here as the developmental stages do not correspond with the other learning to learn capacities as described here. Coding is explained in detail the relevant chapter.

Developmental framework

Learning to learn capacities

	Stage 1: Early From around 24 months to 36 months	**Stage 2: Active** From 36 months, up to and around 48 months	**Stage 3: Mature** From 48 months, up to and around 60 months
Matching	Making pairs of two identical objects	Matching the model by actively seeking and making comparisons	The best fit selecting by looking and making mental comparisons
Sorting	Separating identical objects into sets	Creating sets by sorting collections of objects or picture cards	Classifying according to a variety of attributes
Seriation	Chaining objects in long rows	**a.** Alternating sequence of objects **b.** Getting bigger or smaller in size using 3-D objects	**a.** Creating repeating patterns with objects or pictures **b.** Organising into size order, building up and along
Drawing	Making a mark with a tool	Drawing lines on paper in different directions and patterns	Drawing shapes and pictures and observing in order to copy
Brick-building	Piling with lots of different materials	Planning to build and doing so with purpose; the model might not resemble the stated plan	Copying and building by analysing a model as well as designing his own structures

Teaching the learning to learn capacities

In the following chapters, all the learning to learn capacities will be described in detail, outlining the achievements at every stage.

There is a description of the teaching strategies, equipment and general set up which follows the recommendations for the structured teaching sessions; the approach is similar for all the learning to learn capacities.

Use the developmental framework to establish the approximate stages of development within each learning to learn capacity.

The activity section is divided into the three developmental stages, with ideas for games to play:

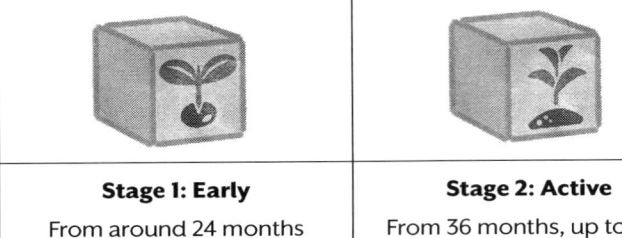

Stage 1: Early	Stage 2: Active	Stage 3: Mature
From around 24 months to 36 months	From 36 months, up to and around 48 months	From 48 months, up to and around 60 months

Variations are described for many of the activities. These are essential: the child needs a broad spectrum of experiences to build firm foundations.

The variations can be adapted and expanded in response to the child's interest and the available material. Use your imagination to create new games and variations; there is no right or wrong. When a child is enjoying himself, you are getting the level right.

> ## Cora
>
> Cora is a teenager; she is very good at routine tasks like finishing a puzzle, copying a set pattern or stacking the nesting cups. These are all familiar tasks, she knows how to complete them all without help from anyone; once done, she is done, and she gets up.
>
> Cora does not learn anything new from going through the repetitive routines of completing these quick, set activities. To broaden her experiences, several variations were introduced:
>
> - The puzzle pieces were hidden in boxes, plastic folders etc. Cora practised her fine motor skills and problem-solving to find them.
> - She liked patterns; the variations incorporated different levels of difficulty and using a new collection of materials to create the patterns.
> - Turn-taking was introduced, Cora created her own pattern which the adult copied, and then the roles were reversed.
> - She practised her ability to order according to size by sorting out the kitchen cupboard.
>
> Cora encountered many new learning opportunities in this way; she was able to stay engaged for much longer and she became much more flexible in coping with demands.

MATCHING

Definition

"This cognitive capacity is defined as 'the process of finding the least difference between two objects and the active placing of them together."

Geoffrey Waldon refined the commonly used term, matching, and gave his own meaning to the concept. Matching does not mean making pairs of identical objects or pictures, but it refers to the **mental processes of making comparisons** between objects or patterns. It is an active process and many comparisons are made, and countless possible matches will be discounted before the final decision; these two are the best fit to make a pair as they are the least different. According to Waldon, the child must first learn to match and then match to learn; it is an essential cognitive processing tool.

Links

Matching and sorting have a common origin in picking up and putting in but they become two distinctly different mental capacities. Both employ the techniques of identifying the characteristics of the objects or patterns, and noticing their similarities and differences. However, from these observations two separate processing tools emerge: when sorting, the focus is on the features the objects have in common and will serve to define a set or category; in contrast, when matching, the focus is on the differences between two objects: are they too different from one another or can they be seen as a pair?

Everyday matching

Finding a pair of socks is an obvious example of everyday matching, as is locating a pair of shoes in the big pile under the stairs. As adults, we may go to the shop to find a replacement for a broken mug and buy one which is as similar to the original as we can find, despite not being identical. An adult will be applying the processes of matching when he is looking at a cooking recipe which requires sweet potatoes but there are none in the cupboard; however, there is a butternut squash and the decision is, are the two vegetable sufficiently similar so that one can be substituted for the other? The concept of matching is also constantly employed in learning, for example in order to read the child must be able to match letters and recognise that letters written in different fonts are still the same letters. The early number skills require the recognition of patterns such as 'two-ness', two blocks, two lines, two spots etc., all represent the quantity of two. These are just a few examples of the mental processes of matching applied in everyday learning.

Development of matching

Matching can be described in three broad stages, which develop gradually alongside the other learning capacities.

Stage 1. Early matching: Making pairs

This is referred to as **pairing** and it is defined as bringing together two identical objects. At this stage, which normally happens between 18 months to two years, the child can pick up two identical objects that are presented side by side; when he is shown one object, he can find the match if this is within his field of vision. At this time the child's verbal understanding is growing and he can for example search for an object he has been asked for, such as 'give me the car'. It is not part of the learning to learn approach to make verbal requests, the focus is on the perception and understanding of the characteristics of the objects.

The child can be taught the pairing game, and once he understands the convention, this game is used to extend his understanding of matching through many new experiences. The game is an exercise in scanning and focusing on specific objects, making mental comparisons and being able to discount some pieces in order to select the match which makes the pair.

Stage 2. Active matching: Matching the model

Active matching happens when the child understands that he is deliberately looking for a match to a model which he has been shown. He can scan around, he can select one object and ignore the rest; he can do so without any physical prompt. The child is still using the technique of bringing the match to the model to prove or compare, 'Do I think this is the right one?' The child is learning to match, first with identical pairs and later playing with pairs of non-identical objects, such as two cups with different patterns or two similar but different keys.

As the comprehension of the matching processes grows, the ability to look for similarities and differences in pictures and patterns emerges. The child can distinguish and match simple monochrome drawings. He can focus on the essence and ignore redundant information; take for example a set of cards with different shapes: the colours of the outlines vary but this is an irrelevant detail and should be discounted; the focus is the shape itself. Other examples of redundant information when matching shapes are variations in their size, added colour or some background distractions like dots.

Stage 3. Mature matching: The best fit

The child can now match unassisted; he can look at a number of models, compare and contrast and make his own decisions. Mature matching is the ability to work from one model, to hold this image in mind and look around, make mental comparisons and decide which is the best match. A child might select two pieces to make a pair, but he may later change this decision when he notices a better fit; it is during this active process of deliberating that the learning takes place.

The child now understands the processes of matching. The ability to attend to specific details and distinguish between various features in pictures or graphic patterns, is an ongoing development which continues throughout life.

Teaching techniques

General set-up

Matching is one element of the learning to learn session and the set-up follows the general guidelines for the lesson. Please note the following advice:

The purpose is to teach the capacity to match as a tool for future learning and not to practise isolated skills such as how to perfect a picture lotto board.

The facilitator uses a physical prompt: this can be either hand over hand, pointing or modelling; there is no verbal instruction during the session.

The session starts with exercises to strengthen the fundamental movement abilities and the continuant capacity, before the matching game is introduced.

It is advisable to start the pairing game by playing with objects before moving onto matching pictures; this gets him thinking about making pairs.

The facilitator sits behind the child during the early stage of teaching the pairing game.

When the child can match independently, the facilitator can stand up and move around; this enables her to scatter the objects or pictures over a larger area, and this encourages active searching by the child.

Role of the facilitator

It is a good idea to play several different matching games within a session as well as introducing changes to how these are played. The repetitions help to increase the child's focus and sustained attention. Variations which can strengthen the thinking processes include:

- ▶ Place the cards upside down.
- ▶ Spread the cards over a wide area.
- ▶ Include surplus cards which have to be considered then discounted in the process.
- ▶ Place a few obstacles in the way like hiding a card under a cup or putting the cards in a small plastic wallet.

The child needs to be taught the convention of playing the matching game, here referred to as the pairing game; the steps are described below in Making pairs. It takes time for the child to learn how to play the game; give him all the help he needs at all stages in this learning process. The child should not feel he is being tested.

If the child does not find the match and chooses something completely different, simply put this object back on the table.

Next, hold the model beside the intended match and guide him to pick it up.

Learning to play the pairing game is the first step in teaching the processes of matching. The children might become confident and competent at playing these matching games but find it difficult to apply these abilities in everyday life. Their matching skills must be generalised and incorporated into everyday learning situations.

MATCHING ACTIVITIES

STAGE 1. EARLY MATCHING
Making pairs

The main equipment needed is a collection of pairs of identical objects: they all need to be quite different in form, size and colour. It is preferable to use 'scrap' objects such as corks, wooden discs, bottle tops, rings, empty spice jars etc. because they have very little inherent interest to the child and are therefore less likely to distract him from the purpose of the game of making pairs.

All the activities described here at stage one, lead towards independent matching. Some children learn the game quickly whereas others take longer and they need to go through all the steps slowly, many times over. There is no need to follow the instructions rigidly; adapt and adjust in response to the child and move on when he is ready.

Placing the pairs together

EQUIPMENT: Set of five identical pairs of objects.

ACTIVITY: This describes the first step in teaching the pairing game, simply picking up a partner in each hand and placing them together. The adult is fully supporting every action with hand over hand help. Set the game up with the pairs placed together, spaced around on the table.

Step 1. Guide the child to pick up one partner, immediately followed by picking up the twin in the other hand.

Step 2. Place the pair together, somewhere else on the table.

Step 3. Repeat this process for all the pairs.

Step 4. Continue for a while until all the pairs have been picked up and moved to new positions on the table.

Together we find the match

EQUIPMENT: Set of five or six identical pairs.

ACTIVITY: Prepare the game by separating the pairs, placing half of each on the table, and keeping the stock of the twins to one side.

Step 1. Present one object in the open hand, then prompt the child to pick up the match and place it in the open palm; now he has made a pair.

Step 2. The pair is placed together on the table.

Step 3. These two steps are repeated to make all the pairs; by the end all the pairs are side by side on the table.

Note: the open hand presenting the object can be moved towards the twin. This will draw the child's attention in that direction if he is unsure.

VARIATION: The facilitator picks up one of a pair and shows it to the child. Next, she prompts the child to pick up the twin and place it in the open hand. The pair is then removed from the table. Repeat until all the pairs are gathered in.

I can find the match on my own

EQUIPMENT: Set of five or six identical pairs.

ACTIVITY: Use the pairing set from the previous game and add an extra pair or two. Spread all the objects randomly on the table which means the partners are now placed apart.

Step 1. The facilitator picks up one object and presents it to the child in her open hand. Give the child time to look at this piece and scan around to find the match. After a while, help him to pick up the match and pass it over.

Step 2. Place both pieces back on the table; set them apart so they are now in a different location.

Step 3. Repeat the first two steps of presenting one object and finding the match, returning them to a new position every time.

Observe the child carefully: can he focus on the model and look around and locate the partner? Can he pick it up and pass it over? Find the right level of support to ensure that the child succeeds. Whilst the aim is for the child to complete the task on his own, the adult may intermittently step in to help.

VARIATIONS:
a. Use a different collection of pairs.
b. Play the game with more pairs.

Lots of pairs

EQUIPMENT: Large collection of 10 or more identical pairs.

ACTIVITY: Increase the number of pairs and spread them over a wider space. This will encourage the child to look around.

Step 1. The facilitator presents a model in her open hand and the child finds the match and gives it to her.

Step 2. The pairs are returned to the table, placed apart and in different positions; the game is repeated many times over.

VARIATIONS:
a. Place some obstacles in the way so the child has to be really active when looking around: in, under or behind boxes or trays, on the floor or the table nearby.

b. Present the model in different places, by the side, up high, down low!

Can the child look for a piece without being distracted by the other objects around?

STAGE 2. ACTIVE MATCHING
Matching the model

At this stage, the child understands the concept of matching: he has to find the partner to a model by actively seeking and making comparisons; he can do this without help. The active matching games are similar to the pairing games but they incorporate more variations to strengthen his understanding of the matching process. The H-board is introduced as a tool for matching and this will be described later in this section.

At this stage, two collections of object pairs are needed:

- **Set 1:** A large collection of identical pairs.
- **Set 2:** A collection of non-identical pairs, but sufficiently similar to be perceived as a pair, such as two different corks, a round and a hexagonal jam jar lid, two different keys, a red and a green milk-bottle tops etc.

Give-me!

EQUIPMENT: Set 1, the large collection of identical pairs.

ACTIVITY: The aim is to teach the meaning of the open hand, 'give-me gesture' alongside showing an object in the other hand. This is an important skill, for the child to look at the object in the adult's hand and to understand he is required to find the matching piece and place it in her other hand. This can only be achieved once he is independently picking up the play pieces.

Some children learn this quickly, others need to practise the game for a while. The suggested teaching sequence can be shortened or lengthened with more steps to scaffold the learning; it all depends on the individual child.

Step 1. Spread about eight pairs randomly on the table.

Step 2. The facilitator picks up one object, holds it in her open hand. She moves this hand near the match on the table.

Step 3. The 'give-me' gesture is made with the other hand next to the match. The child might initially need some guidance to understand the gesture as a request.

Step 4. When the child has given the adult the match, she places the two objects together as a pair on the table.

Step 5. Repeat steps two to four, until all the pairs are made.

Look around for the match

EQUIPMENT: Set 1, the large collection of identical pairs.

ACTIVITY: This activity is the natural extension of learning the meaning of the 'Give-me' gesture. When the child responds consistently in the game above, this activity is a variation which increases the child's capacity to focus, to look around and to make decisions.

Step 1. Spread the large collection of pairs randomly on the table.

Step 2. The facilitator shows one object and makes the give-me gesture some distance from the match.

Step 3. The child focuses on the model, finds the match and places it in the open hand.

Step 4. Both pieces are placed back on the table. The game continues and can be ongoing because the pieces are constantly moved around.

Look closely: which two pieces can make a pair?

EQUIPMENT: Set 2: the collection of non-identical pairs.

ACTIVITY: This game is played in the same way as 'Look around for the match' described above. This time play with a set of non-identical pairs.

Step 1. Spread the collection of pairs on the table; use eight to ten pairs.

Step 2. The facilitator shows the model and makes the 'give-me' gesture with the other hand. The aim is for the child to find the match on his own.

Step 3. If the child cannot locate the match, hold the model next to it and repeat the give-me gesture.

Step 4. The pair is returned to the table, apart and in new positions. The game continues.

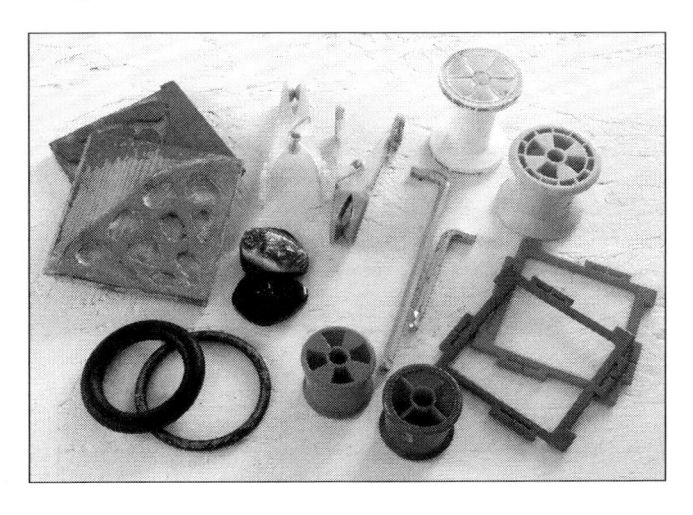

Keep matching with variations

EQUIPMENT: Large collection of pairs, both identical and non-identical.

ACTIVITY: The aim is to secure the child's ability to match by practising the mental processes involved: focusing, looking around, making mental comparisons and coming to a decision. Play the game as described above and use a greater number and variety of pairs.

VARIATIONS: Variations should be introduced gradually, only one at a time and maybe later combined, until eventually the child can cope with any and all of them.

- Increase the number of pairs.
- Show the model in different positions by moving around: to the left, on the right, up high or down low, in front or behind.
- The give-me hand is presented in new positions.
- Speed up the game: make the requests quickly, one after the other.

The model can be shown quickly, then hidden out of view by turning the hand away. If the child didn't catch it the first time, present it again.

Spread the pieces over a wider area and place some slightly out of the child's field of vision.

Place obstacles in the way such as hiding the pieces in, on or under each other, in plastic saucers or small boxes, so the child has to be effortful in his search.

Picture matching

EQUIPMENT: Set of five or six pairs of picture cards with simple patterns, all looking very different from each other.

ACTIVITY: Picture matching games can be played in the same way as object matching. However, when the pictures are introduced, it is wise to go through the initial teaching sequence for early matching, before progressing towards the ability to play 'Look around for the match' as described earlier in this section. The child is likely to need extra help at the point of changing from playing with objects to matching pictures.

Step 1. Spread the cards on the table. The facilitator picks up a picture card, holds it in her open hand and makes the give-me gesture with the other, next to the matching card.

Step 2. Guide the child to pick it up and place it in the open hand.

Step 3. Place the pair together on the table.

Step 4. Repeat steps 1 to 3 until all the matches have been made; fade the prompt when the child can locate and pick up the card independently.

VARIATIONS: **a.** Spread the cards around on the table and repeat the game; every time a pair is made, the two cards are returned to the table in different positions.

b. Increase the number of pairs in the collection.

Can the child actively search for a match until he succeeds?

Introducing the H-board

The H-board is a matching board originally designed by Geoffrey Waldon. It is a long board with wooden facings which create well defined spaces; the picture cards or small objects can be placed in pairs and they can easily be moved and swapped around. The board is used with children who have reached the active matching level: it is a simple aid to structure the activities.

The first step is to teach the child how to play games on this board. It is a skill in itself, knowing the convention of how to place the pairs side by side and having the ability to scan the board. It is important to take time to ensure the child is completely familiar with this process of playing matching games, only then can it be used as a teaching tool.

The list below describes the increasing levels of competence in playing games on the H-board. Some steps will need to be repeated several times before the child's understanding is secure, others can be passed over quickly. In this description, picture cards are used, but it is advisable to practise with small objects as well.

Use a set of matching cards with simple, clear illustrations. The facilitator places one of a pair on the board, starting in the top, left corner; she gives the child the matching card and points to the place underneath, indicating that he should place the card in that space. Continue along to fill the board, making one pair at a time.

Empty the H-board, one half to the top, the matching half tipped off below the H-board; the cards are roughly in the same order. The facilitator starts in the top corner, places the first card back on the board; she points to the space underneath, indicating to the child to place the matching card. Give a little physical guidance if needed; continue to fill the board, one pair at a time.

Lay out half the set in the top row and give the child one of the matching cards. Encourage him to run this along the row, back and forth, so he is actively comparing two cards at a time; let him make the decision where to place it. Continue until the board is complete.

Fill the top row and spread the matching cards on the table; encourage the child to pick up one at a time and find the match. The target is for the child to continue and complete the board on his own.

STAGE 3. MATURE MATCHING
The best fit

At this level the child can match independently, he can look at a number of possible matches, compare and contrast and make his decision. 'These two make a pair, they are not the same but the fit is good enough!'

The new developments at this stage are the abilities to:

- ▶ Look at a specific card on the board.
- ▶ Scan the collection which is spread widely around.
- ▶ Choose a match.

These skills can be taught through a rigid routine of pointing and looking. The guidance below is very specific and detailed, but it may not be necessary to be so systematic and repetitive; take the lead from the child and move on when he is ready.

Lay out the cards on the top row and spread the matching cards on the table.

Prompt both the child's hands, and with his left and right index finger, point to the first card on the top left. Next move one pointing finger to the empty space below to indicate where the matching card should go; keep this finger in place. With the other hand start to hover and search for the matching card, pick it up and place it to complete the pair.

Repeat the double pointing, moving the pointing finger from top to bottom and searching with the other hand; continue until the board is completed.

The process is key: focusing, remembering and searching for one specific card; the child might pick up a card, bring it to the model, compare and reject it and return it to the table.

If a child chooses a card which is not a good match, leave it as placed for a while and observe: will he change his mind? If an out-of-place card seems to cause agitation, simply remove it and return it to the table.

Phase out the prompt to point, aiming for the child to continue independently.

Gradually increase the number of cards the child has to scan, e.g. introduce rogue cards which have to be discounted when the child is mentally making the comparisons.

More variations include the use of a wider space; place cards out of reach; turn some upside down or half hidden under cups etc.

Can the child work systematically along the board and make the pairs?

Specific understanding of patterns and pictures

The child has now learnt to match and from this point onwards, the activities should focus on matching to learn. Matching cards are a convenient method to create new experiences, they can be devised to introduce a variety of challenges. The examples below are arranged developmentally, with a brief description of the specific abilities involved in processing the information at each level. It is advisable to design many different exercises at each level to provide a wide range of learning experiences.

Level 2 Active matching

Matching simple pictures or graphic patterns, all very different in appearance.

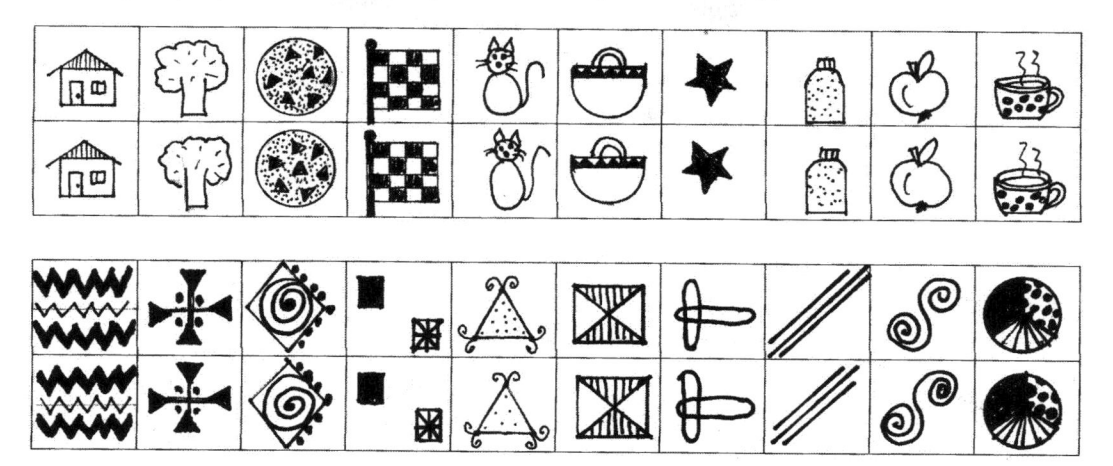

Simple monochrome shapes, no colour or other added features.

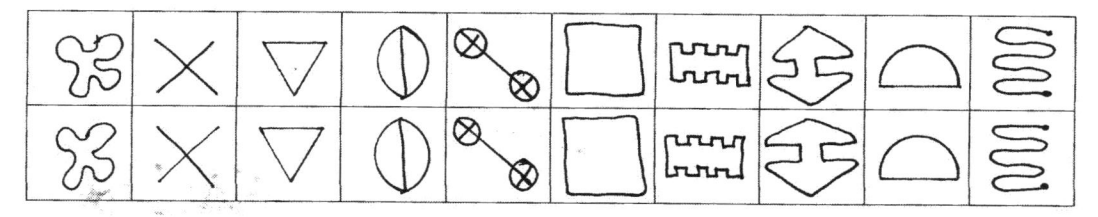

Match the shapes and ignoring other details as they are irrelevant, for example:

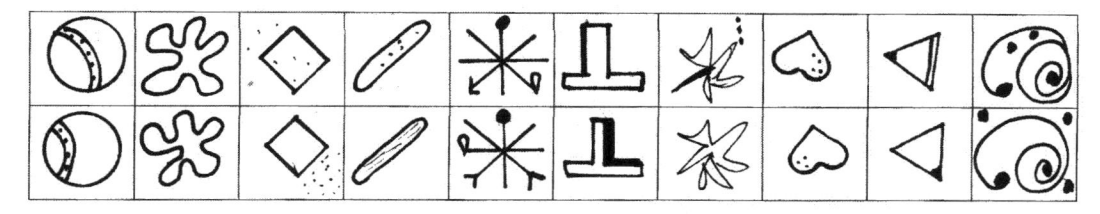

Pay attention to the shapes; in this set the character of the line is irrelevant.

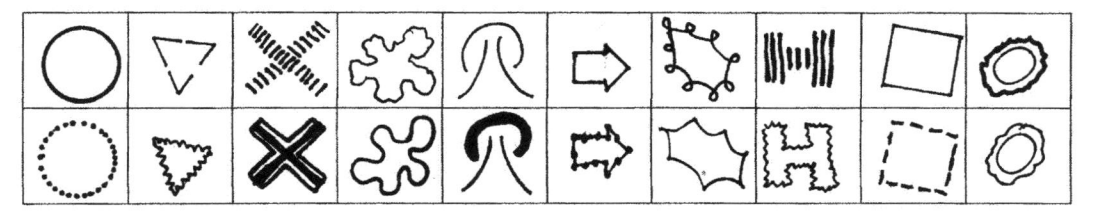

Ignore the background and focus on the picture or the shape.

SECTION 3: PRACTICAL ACTIVITIES

In this example, the shapes are different in size, but they still make pairs.

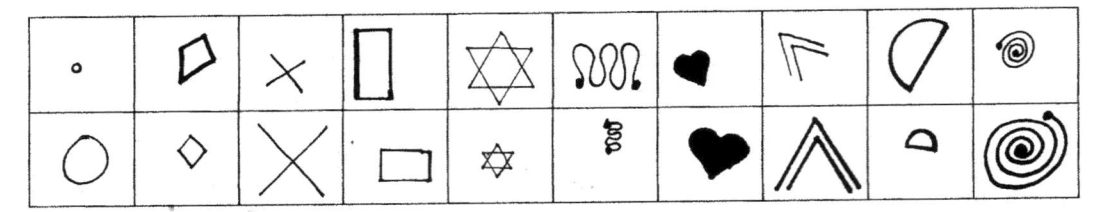

Level 3 Mature matching

It is necessary to consider two separate elements such as shape and pattern, or shape and colour. It is not sufficient to base the decision on looking at just one of the elements.

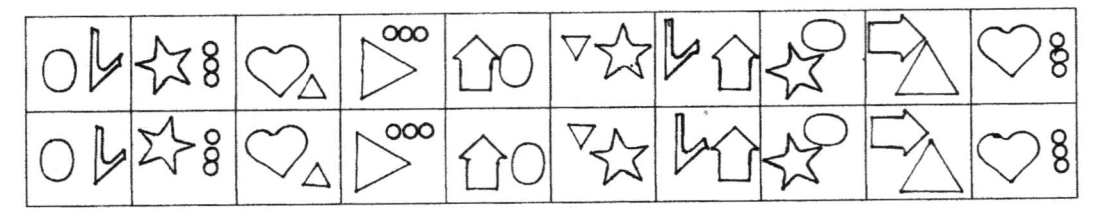

Matching overlapping shapes requires the ability to see the two shapes as separate.

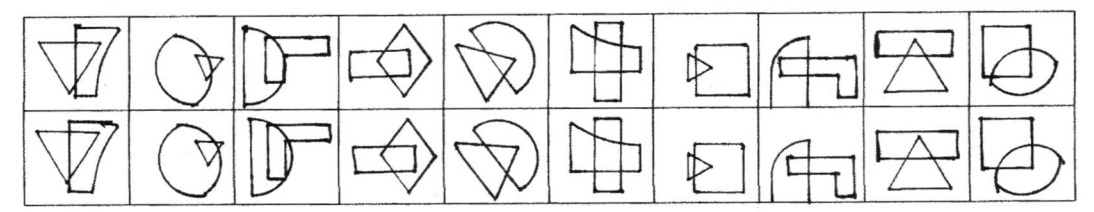

Figures or shapes can be presented at different angles; it requires the ability to attend to the orientation and find a figure that is similar.

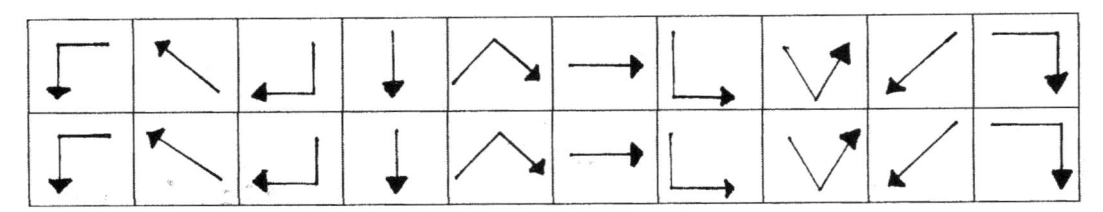

The visual ability to match can be practised by looking for small details and variations, this is an important part of using matching as a learning tool.

The ability to discount irrelevant information is important: it means noticing and understanding what is important and the rest can be ignored.

High-level matching involves matching by association: things that go together or belong together can make a pair. The pairings can be temporary and change with the context.

This requires a sophisticated understanding of the world.

SECTION 3: PRACTICAL ACTIVITIES

SORTING

As a child explores, he begins to notice how things can be grouped together; some objects have certain features in common: for example, some things feel rough, some objects roll and others have corners etc. He might discover that long objects are good for prodding and he decides to collect them together and stick them in the sand; stones and shells are hard but different so he decides to collect them into two separate buckets. These groupings can be changed as he becomes aware of other characteristics; this is the beginning of sorting.

Definition

> *Sorting is the mental capacity to identify and group together objects which have common characteristics and this leads to the understanding of classification.*

Geoffrey Waldon used the term sorting to describe two distinct levels of mental processing. The first stage is having the ability to look at objects or pictures and allocate them to a set, such as sets of a) buttons, b) coins, c) pieces of wood, d) triangles, e) spoons, f) cubes, g) stones, h) conkers and so on. These sets are based on observable features and concrete experience.

The second, higher-level understanding, is the ability to recognise a set as a category or classification: these are more abstract concepts that grow with experience. Take, for example, the following three ways of classifying a collection: a) roundness, b) edible and c) man-made; the child must have explored widely and acquired a broad understanding of the world in order to do this. Several of the objects could potentially belong in more than one set and the child will have to consider the attributes and the options available. A digestive biscuit can belong in all three categories: it is round, edible and man-made!

Sorting is an active process that involves flexible thinking: the child will allocate an object to a set, but he may later change his mind and move it elsewhere. The critical time for learning is at the point of making the decision, later reviewing this initial choice and a potential change of mind. At the early stages of sorting, the process does not involve verbal labelling of the characteristics or the sets, this is a later development.

Links

The close links in the origin of matching and sorting were described in the previous chapter on matching; the two learning to learn capacities build on the child's early experiences of exploring the properties and characteristics of the objects around, but then the mental processes diverge. When the child is sorting, he thinks about organising the information in his mind according to groups with common features, whereas matching is mentally looking for two that are similar enough to make a pair, and discounting the rest. In other words, during sorting, the mental processes relate to what can be included in a group, the matching process focuses on excluding possible candidates.

SECTION 3: PRACTICAL ACTIVITIES

Everyday sorting

Sorting is involved in many everyday activities, from tidying the cutlery in the kitchen drawers, arranging the food in the fridge and cupboards, to much more specific classification systems like the aisles and shelves in the supermarket, play lists on the phone or the books in the library: sorting is our daily tool for organising.

Development of sorting

Learning to sort can for convenience be described as a progression through three stages. Early sorting is separating, active sorting involves creating sets and thirdly, mature sorting is concerned with classifying; the capacity continues to grow throughout life.

Stage 1. Early sorting: Separating

This is the ability to separate objects into two or three sets, each set being distinctly different from the others, as for example a) curtain rings, b) bulldog clips and c) dice.

Once the child is able to allocate the objects without support from an adult, it is time to introduce the concept of similarity; this means grouping together items which are very similar but not completely identical, for example separating into three sets of a) similar beads, b) a collection of coins and c) fir-cones, varying in size.

At this stage the child is usually ready for activities with sorting cards, separating identical pictures or graphic patterns into sets.

Stage 2. Active sorting: Creating sets

The progression from separating to creating sets involves two significant developments:

1. The child can decide about the 'best fit' for where an object belongs.
2. He begins to create new sets of his own accord.

The child may not yet be consciously aware of the reasons for his decisions; when he is looking and assessing an object, he might change his mind several times.

This development can be illustrated with an example. The child has a mixed collection of objects which fall roughly into three sets; the adult has seeded two trays (she has placed a couple of pieces from the sets in the trays) and left one tray empty. What normally happens at this stage, is the child picks out all the same objects from one category and places them in the seeded tray; he then starts to collect together the second set and notices some objects do not seem to belong. The big step forward is when he creates a new category in the empty tray; in other words, he has decided that some pieces did not fit and he starts a new set.

The child can now accept an object that does not quite fit his criteria for a category and in so doing, he expands his definition of the sets; his understanding of what constitutes a set has broadened. He also pays more attention to the details and he may create subsets within the original groupings. During a game, this ability will be demonstrated as follows: an activity is designed to sort a collection into three sets: a) coloured beads, b) Multilink cubes and c) wooden blocks. Whilst the child is busily sorting, he starts to focus on one particular colour and he decides to make a set of 'red'; he groups together everything red whether they are beads, Multilink or wooden blocks. This could be in a separate tray or a set within a set; the rest of the objects are sorted according to the original criteria. The child's decision shows how actively he is thinking about the task: he is neither right nor wrong, his allocation should be accepted and not interfered with.

At this stage, the child can confidently work with sorting cards which is comparable to sorting objects, but it offers another way of creating new experiences. The ability to sort graphic patterns and picture references develops simultaneously. The child can ignore irrelevant details and variations in the patterns and focus on the salient features.

Stage 3. Mature sorting: Classifying

True mature sorting happens when a child has the ability to define a category and later change his mind to extend or alter the category; sorting has now become a tool for learning.

At this stage, the child learns to apply his own criteria and he also begins to understand that sets can overlap and they can be changed.

The process of classification involves the ability to focus on several characteristics and to decide which are the relevant features in this situation and ignore the rest. A mixed collection of objects can usually be sorted in several ways by changing the primary focus; take as an example a collection of figures designed with many different features: they vary in gender, stance (sitting, standing, bending), in pattern on their clothes (plain, stripy, dots), hair style (long, short, pony tail), hair colour (blond, brown and black) and skin colour (light, dark). This collection can be sorted into many different sets, focusing on only one or two main features, a) hair colour or b) stance, a) gender or b) clothes, a) hair style or b) skin colour etc. This illustrates the multiple ways that categories can be defined. In one instance, certain characteristics are relevant, others are not, then the criteria are altered and the focus has shifted.

The most advanced sorting is called intersectional sorting, and this refers to the ability to consider several criteria simultaneously and understand that sets can overlap. The following example illustrates high level sorting: three categories a) means of transport, b) things that fly and c) toys. There are many overlapping elements here: an aeroplane is a means of transport and it can also fly; a kite can fly and it is also a toy; a car can be a toy as well as a means of transport. The teaching of intersectional sorting often uses the convention of the Venn diagram as well as a matrix.

At the mature sorting stage, the child has learnt to sort: he is now sorting to learn. Present him with a wealth of different experiences to challenge his understanding and this will provide many enjoyable learning opportunities.

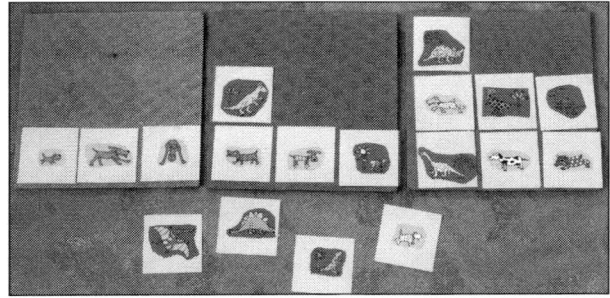

Teaching techniques

General set-up

Sorting is taught in the latter part of the structured learning session, after the thorough practice of the fundamental movement abilities and games involving the continuant capacity. Bear in mind the following points:

- It is important to practise separating with many different collections. Work with three or four at a time.
- When the term 'seed the tray' is used, it refers to placing a few pieces in the tray to indicate the category.
- When separating activities are introduced, the facilitator should sit behind the child to provide the necessary support, moving the objects around and placing them.
- Reduce the support as soon as the child shows signs of carrying on independently.

The role of the facilitator

The facilitator's task is to teach the child the processes of sorting; the activities start with physical guidance of the hands and no verbal instructions. From the stage of active sorting, the child becomes able to continue on his own, and it will be appropriate to sit or stand next to the child.

Equipment

Object collections

Make collections of everyday items such as milk bottle tops, drink bottle tops, corks, stones, shells, jam jar lids, curtain rings, coins, keys, buttons etc. These sets can be identical or there may be some variations: for example, milk bottle tops come in several colours. The sets with variations can be used for sorting according to different criteria.

There are many commercially available sorting sets such as elephants, bears, people or dinosaurs. Colour is often a strong element and for many children this is such a dominant attribute that they cannot focus on the other characteristics. The commercial sets have other limitations, especially at the mature sorting stage: the categories are integral to the sets so the child does not have the opportunity to create his own categories. Finally, small figures easily become toys to be played with instead of sorting; that can become quite a distraction!

Sorting cards

There are some commercially available card-sorting games and they usually focus on colour, shape and number. It is easy to make your own sorting cards from pieces of sturdy card, a pack of stickers and some felt-tip pens; ideas for pictures and patterns corresponding to the different stages of development are included at the end of the activities section.

Containers

Use shallow trays to ensure the child can see what is inside, e.g. large flowerpot saucers or small food trays. The shapes of the containers are unimportant, but use a variety to encourage flexibility of thinking.

Sorting boards

Geoffrey Waldon designed wooden sorting boards with three by three grids. They are a simple way of organising sorting with cards.

SORTING ACTIVITIES

STAGE 1. EARLY SORTING
Separating

The child is taught the skills of separating which means learning to group objects into distinct sets: there is a right set in which each object belongs. Once the child is discriminating and placing the objects on his own, small variations should be introduced. This progression is reflected in the order of the activities below.

Separating two sets

EQUIPMENT: Two distinctly different sets such as a) fir cones and b) coins.

Two shallow trays.

ACTIVITY: **Step 1.** Seed the two trays with a few cones and coins; present one object at a time and support the child with a physical prompt to place it in the correct tray.

Step 2. Repeat the exercise, this time changing the position of the trays. Reduce the amount of support given to the child in line with his responses.

VARIATIONS: **a.** Present the pieces to the child in different places on the table so he has to look around to locate them.

b. Repeat the activity using two different sets of objects.

SECTION 3: PRACTICAL ACTIVITIES

Separating three or more sets

EQUIPMENT: Three to five distinctly different sets such as a) bottle tops, b) rings, c) bricks, d) conkers and e) clothes pegs.

Five trays.

ACTIVITY: **Step 1.** Start with three trays and seed them; present one object at a time and support the child with hand over hand to ensure it is placed correctly.

Step 2. Add an extra seeded tray and start to include these new elements; the child has to look more closely before placing. Fade out the support.

VARIATIONS: **a.** The position of the trays and the delivery of each item, can be altered during the game; this will encourage active looking, both in the picking up and placing.

b. Repeat the activity above with different sets of objects.

c. Play the game with up to five different sorts.

Separating sets and correcting the adult's 'mistake'

EQUIPMENT: Several distinctly different sets such as a) elephants, b) Multilink, c) crayons, d) bottle tops, e) pegs and f) metal bolts.

Sorting trays.

ACTIVITY: **Step 1.** Play the game as described above; start with three sets and increase to four or five by placing extra trays on the table.

Step 2. Present one object at a time in various locations **and** also occasionally drop an object into a wrong tray; the hope is that the child will notice and move it to the correct set. It can help to pause and maybe point to the 'odd' object, thereby drawing attention to it. The object can be left in the tray or the adult can demonstrate that it is possible to move it; observe the child closely and decide which is the best step to take to support his learning.

Can the child correct a 'mistake'?

Separating sets of similar objects

EQUIPMENT: Sets of similar objects e.g. a) bottle tops in different colours, b) button collection, c) lolly sticks in different sizes and colour, d) keys, e) pencils.

Sorting trays.

ACTIVITY: **Step 1.** Start with three trays, one seed in each. Give the child one object and point to the tray where it belongs. Repeat with several objects from every set.

Step 2. Gradually stop pointing; now the child is making the decision.

VARIATIONS: Separating into sets can be varied in several ways:

- ▶ Increase the number of trays.
- ▶ Change the objects.

- Alter the location of the trays on the table.
- Speed up/slow down the delivery of the pieces.
- Make a deliberate 'mistake'.

Learning to use the sorting boards

EQUIPMENT: Several collections of small identical objects.

Sorting boards.

ACTIVITY: The aim of this activity is to place each piece within the framed space on the board. This skill, to place objects with care and precision, is essential in order to use the sorting boards as a tool for more advanced activities.

Step 1. Place two sorting boards on the table and seed each with a couple of objects, carefully positioned within the defined spaces.

Step 2. Give the child one piece and point to a space on the correct board.

Step 3. Reduce the pointing prompt as quickly as possible; fill the boards.

VARIATIONS: **a.** Practise as above with two different collections.

b. Repeat the activity with three or more sets.

Separating sets of pictures on the sorting boards

EQUIPMENT: Three very different sets of 9 identical pictures, for example a) clouds ☁, b) spiderwebs 🕸 and c) aeroplanes ✈.

Three sorting boards.

ACTIVITY: **Step 1.** Place the three sorting boards on the table and seed each with a couple of pictures. Give the child one picture at a time, wait; if he hesitates, point to the correct board. The picture should be placed carefully within the square on the board.

Step 2. Continue to fill both boards; reduce the pointing prompt.

VARIATIONS: Practise separating different sets:

Simple, bold patterns e.g. a) ☯, b) ✤, c) ◉, d), ✺ and e) ✠

Identical coloured pictures e.g. a) shoes, b) trees and c) cars

SECTION 3: PRACTICAL ACTIVITIES

Here are two examples of sorting cards used to introduce the concept of sorting with cards rather than objects.

▶ This set has illustrations with simple pictures: they are all very different and easy to distinguish from each other.

▶ Simple graphic patterns such as these are used to practise separating into clearly defined sets; the geometric patterns in each set are very different.

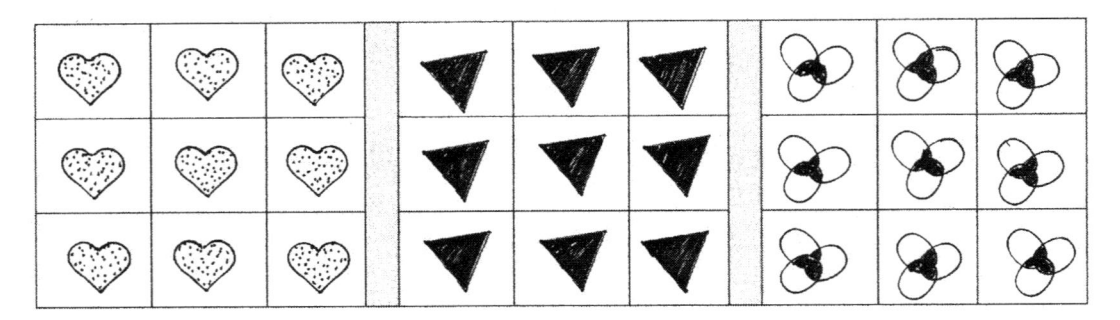

STAGE 2. ACTIVE SORTING
Creating sets

The activities at this stage involve:

▶ Working independently.
▶ Sorting sets of objects or cards.
▶ Grouping objects according to characteristics and disregarding irrelevant details.
▶ Opportunities to define own sets with a mixed collection of objects.
▶ Sorting sets with geometric patterns.
▶ Sorting picture cards into categories.

The activities in this section are arranged developmentally; it is appropriate and necessary to include games from this and earlier stages in order to give the child the broadest possible experiences.

Sorting without help and starting more sets

EQUIPMENT: Three or more collections of non-identical objects, belonging to obvious sets such as a) cubes, b) corks, c) buttons, d) mixed nuts and e) lids.

Sorting trays.

ACTIVITY: **Step 1.** Mix together two sets in a shallow box, set out two sorting trays. Give the child the box, model rummaging through the objects and picking out one element at a time and placing it in a tray.

Step 2. Stop the modelling and encourage the child to continue unsupported.

VARIATIONS: **a.** Once the child is sorting two sets on his own, add another collection of objects to his box and put a new sorting tray on the table. This should encourage him to start a new set.

b. Continue as above, but add a new set whilst the child is still in the process of sorting.

c. Practise this activity with many different objects that are similar but not identical, e.g. metal washers, conkers, variety of wooden beads.

Broadening the definition of a set

EQUIPMENT: Three collections of non-identical objects as for example sets of different a) cylinders, b) rings of wood and metal, c) things made from metal. The emphasis is on observable features.

Sorting trays.

ACTIVITY: **Step 1.** Seed the three trays and introduce one object at a time, chosen because they fit clearly into the categories above, cylinders, rings and metal.

Step 2. Introduce a piece which can belong in either of two sets: a metal cylinder is both metal and a cylinder, which category do I choose? A metal curtain ring is a ring and metal, that could belong in both trays. The child's learning is in his decision-making; accept his decision, though he may choose to move the object later.

VARIATION: Create sets with potential for overlap between the categories, such as plastic spoons, metal and wooden rings. The objects in this collection that will stretch the child's thinking are the metal spoons, metal rings, plastic rings.

SECTION 3: PRACTICAL ACTIVITIES

Sorting simple picture cards

EQUIPMENT: Sets of picture cards, falling into three distinctly different categories e.g. ducks, balls and doors or another set with clouds, ice creams and screw drivers; the pictures in each set look more or less alike, without being identical.

Sorting boards.

ACTIVITY: **Step 1.** Seed the three boards with a card from each category.

Step 2. Give the child one card at a time to place; if he needs help, point to the right board. Mix up the order of presenting the cards so the child has to keep scanning all the boards before making a decision.

VARIATIONS: **a.** Increase the number of sets sorted at any one time.

b. Use sets of pictures which require more attention to the details, such as teddies, dolls and plastic toys or three different animals, cows, cats and giraffes; within each set, the animals look different in colour, size or posture.

c. When the child can confidently carry on without help, give him the stack of cards and let him work his way through them, one after the other.

Sorting graphic patterns

EQUIPMENT: Three sets of cards with simple outlines of shapes e.g. ☽, ◇ and +.

ACTIVITY: The aim is to sort the cards onto the boards without help; pointing to the correct board will to get the activity rolling.

Step 1. Seed the boards with one card from each category.

Step 2. Give the child one card at a time to place on the board and continue till all is done.

VARIATIONS: **a.** Present the cards in different locations so the child must look around to locate it.

b. Change the order and position of the sorting boards on the table.

c. Increase from three to four or more sets; the child has to consider several options before making his decision.

Here are some examples of sorting cards; they are arranged developmentally and illustrate the progression in the understanding of categories. These suggestions can be varied and expanded in numerous ways to give many new experiences at every stage.

a. Here are shapes and pictures with small variations within each set, such as uneven sizes, non-identical pictures or patterns.

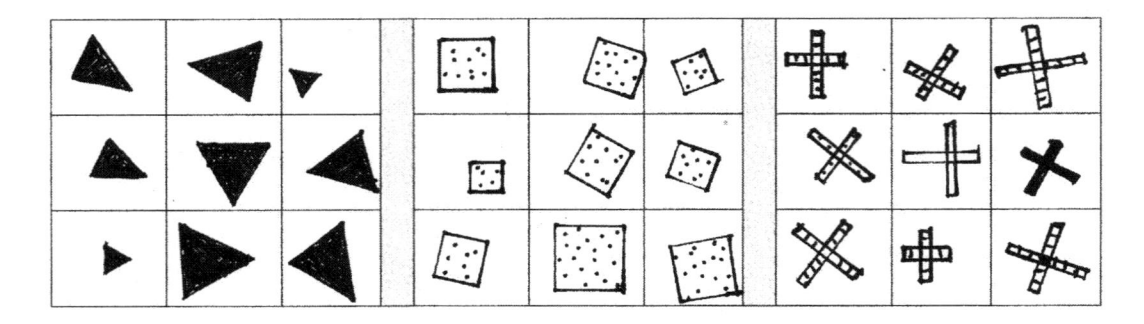

SECTION 3: PRACTICAL ACTIVITIES

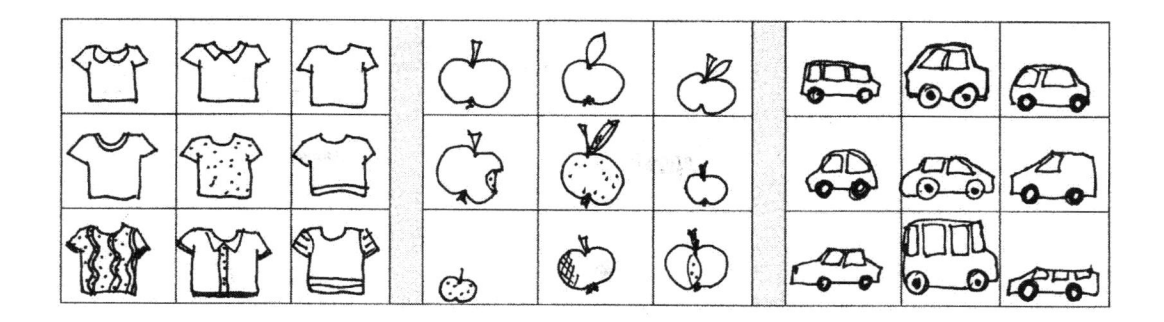

b. Irrelevant details like background pattern can be added to a shape or a picture: this requires the ability to focus on the relevant details and ignore the rest.

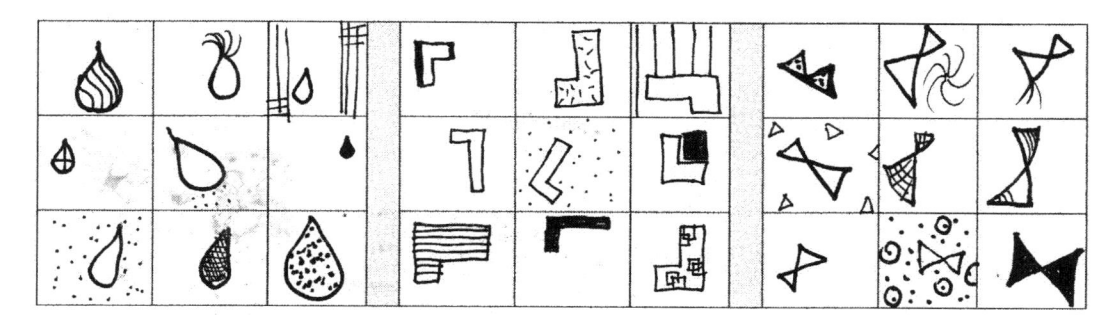

c. In the graphic set, the shapes are distorted and they no longer look the same, yet they still constitute a set. Take, for example, the set based on diamonds, rectangles and circles. The shapes can become so wobbly that a diamond looks almost like a rectangle, so where does it belong? The second example, the picture set, illustrates variations within the groupings, such as the birds, hats and boats are no longer identical pictures.

SECTION 3: PRACTICAL ACTIVITIES

101

d. A set can constitute a collection of fragments and the underlying shape defines the category. The example here is showing fragments of a house, crockery and a train, and each piece has to be allocated to one of the three sets.

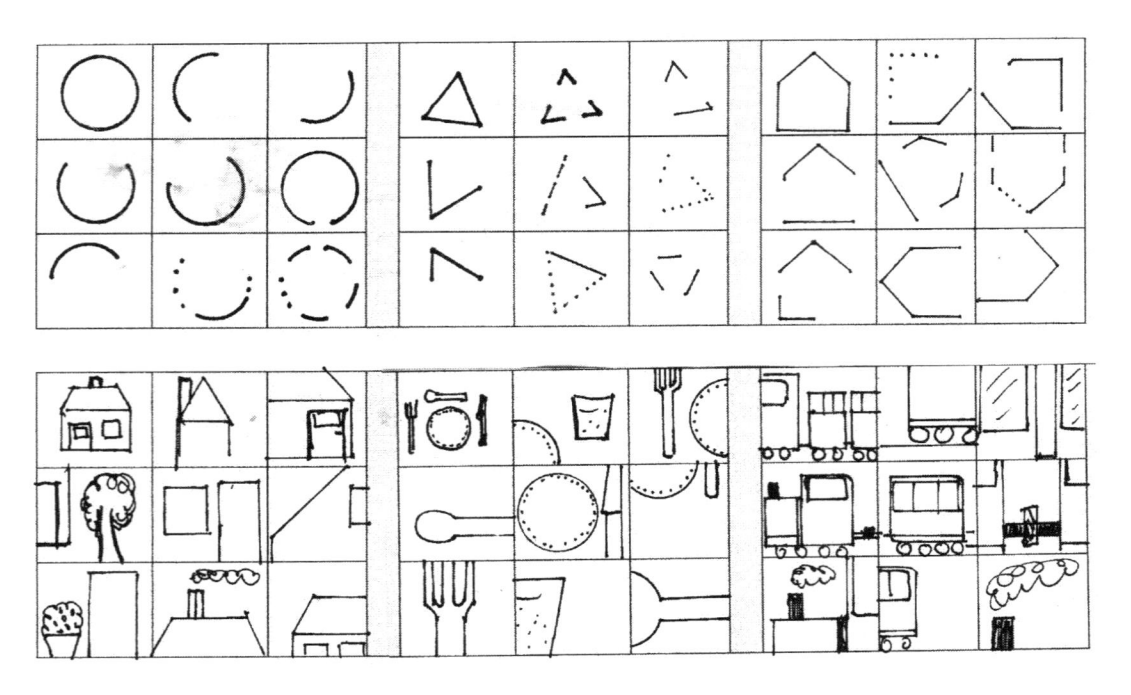

e. The defining picture or shape can be embedded in increasingly complex patterns, and the superfluous information has to be discounted.

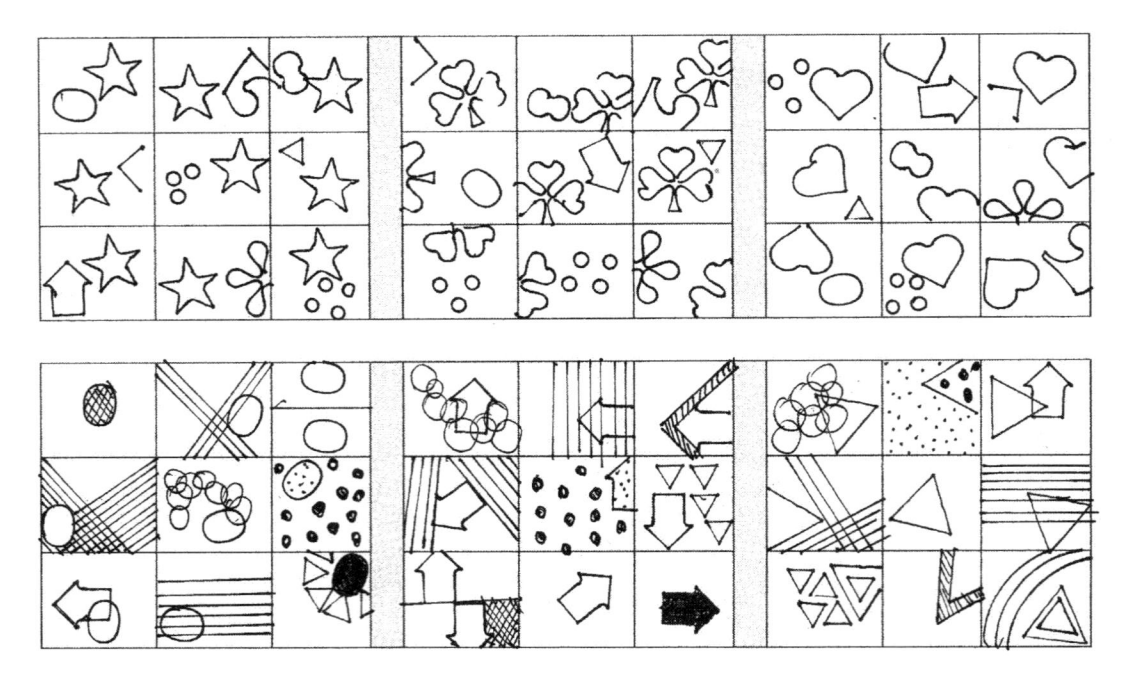

SECTION 3: PRACTICAL ACTIVITIES

STAGE 3. MATURE SORTING
Classifying

The activities at this stage involve:

- ▶ Sorting objects or picture cards into sets by association; this means thinking more abstractly: what does a group have in common? Take, for example, three categories: a) toys, b) clothes or c) tools; these are objects used for different purposes.
- ▶ Consider that categories can overlap, thinking beyond the concrete level of materials or shape. Objects can belong in more than one set, depending on how the parameters are defined.
- ▶ The ability to consider a large number of groupings.
- ▶ The categories can be drawn from real life, and the child's understanding will depend on his experiences.
- ▶ Geometric and abstract patterns, with varying degrees of complexity, can be used to extend the understanding of sorting.

Classification games with objects

EQUIPMENT: Sets of objects with overlapping categories: e.g. money (coins, notes), buttons (metal, plastic, spherical), beads (metal, plastic, glass).

Sorting trays.

ACTIVITY: **Step 1.** Seed each tray with a defining piece. Start with objects which are similar to the 'seed', giving the child one at a time.

Step 2. Gradually introduce the items which could fall into either category, such as a bead-shaped button. Accept the child's decisions.

VARIATIONS: **a.** Create more sets which require careful consideration, for example: batteries (cylinders, cuboid), bricks (cubes, cylinders) and a set of wooden pieces in different shapes.

b. Include a rogue object that doesn't fit anywhere; how does the child deal with that conundrum?

Classification games with sorting cards

Sorting cards are ideal for developing the understanding of how things can be grouped together in many different ways, depending on the context. The concepts relating to the world around and the ability to analyse graphic patterns, develop simultaneously. Play the games with sorting boards and cards, first seeding the boards, then giving the child the cards, one at a time or the whole stack, for him to work his way through. The illustrations here aim to give ideas for variations which can all be further developed.

a. The ideas for categories should relate to the child's experiences. For a young child it might be toys, clothes, food, furniture, houses, animals etc.

b. For older children the categories will be broader and with possible overlaps such as a) living things, b) things that fly and c) insects.

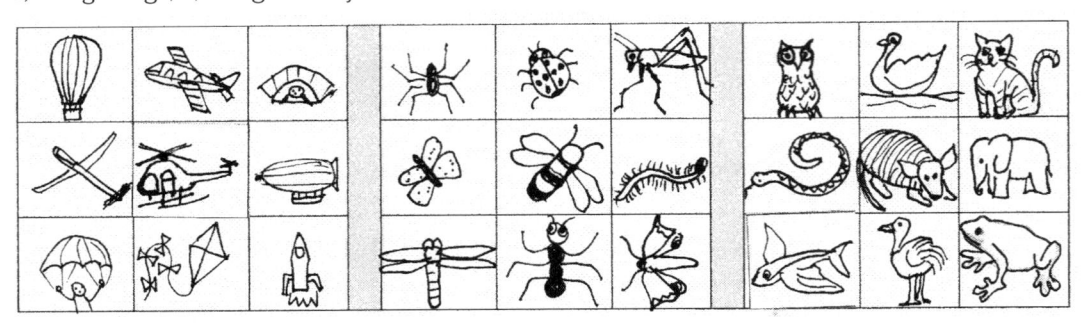

c. Intersectional sorting involves considering two criteria and determine the exact point of overlap between them. In this example, the first criterion is shape, represented by the cards along the top; the second criterion is pattern, and the defining cards are laid out down the side of the matrix. The challenge for the child is to find the exact spot for each card, considering both shape and pattern.

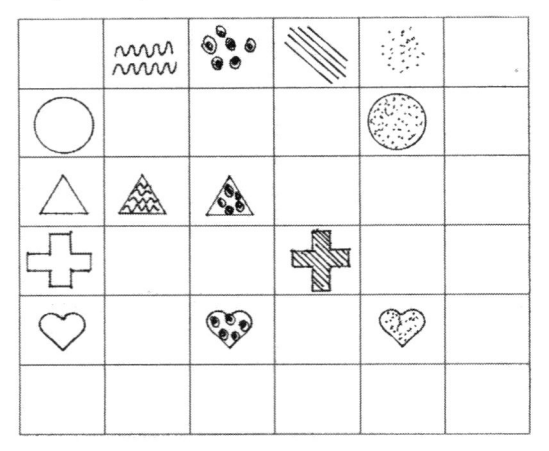

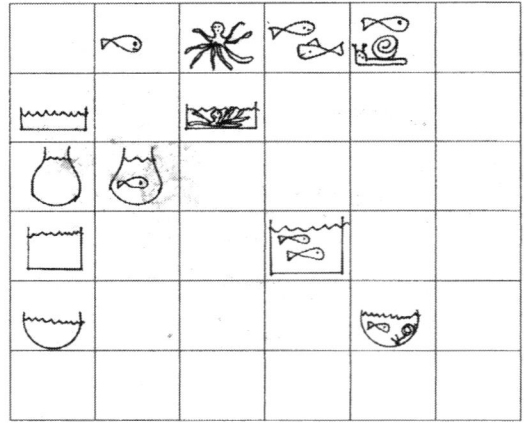

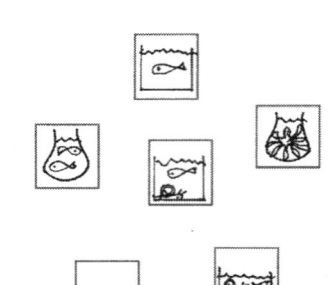

SECTION 3: PRACTICAL ACTIVITIES

SERIATION

Definition

Seriation is the term Waldon chose to describe the concept often referred to as sequencing. He defined seriation as 'the capacity to extrapolate patterns from fragments', this means having the ability to perceive the order within a sequence of events.

There are two types of logical sequences which develop simultaneously, a) repeating series, which relate to repeating patterns such as a chain of (red, blue, green) (red, blue, green) and b) expansive series, which describe sequences increasing or decreasing in size, such as a set of stacking cups or Russian dolls.

Both types of series require the mental ability to recognise the essential elements within them and from these fragments, deduce the overall pattern.

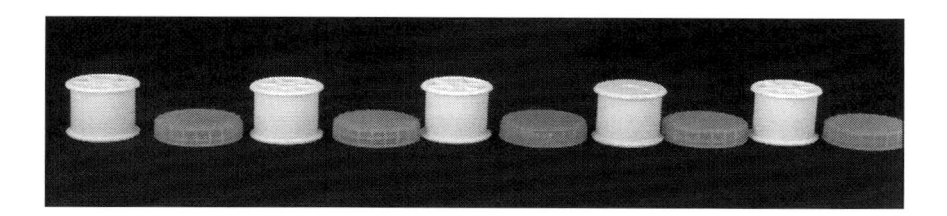

Links

Seriation develops alongside the other learning to learn capacities. In order to understand a pattern, you need to be able to match and find the elements that are the same or very similar. One of the many attributes a child explores when sorting will be the relative size of an object: is it smaller, is it bigger or maybe the same? Another skill which is associated with brick-building, is the ability to position objects together and perceive the space they occupy; this requires an understanding of the relative sizes of the objects such as which is smaller, which is bigger? This illustrates again how the development of the learning to learn capacities are completely interconnected.

SECTION 3: PRACTICAL ACTIVITIES

Everyday seriation

Many everyday tasks involve a sequence of actions such as getting dressed, pants before trousers, t-shirt before jumper, or a bedtime sequence of bath, pyjamas, story, bed and sleep. These types of sequences are built on familiarity and lots of practice, and they help the child to understand that events happen in a certain sequence; there is an inbuilt order to the day.

However, the learning to learn capacity of seriation is quite different to understanding the order of everyday events; seriation refers to the cognitive ability to deduce from a pattern what has gone before, what comes next or what is missing in a sequence. This capacity is applied in many everyday situations such as organising the bowls in the cupboard so they stack up and don't fall down, or in making a bead necklace with coloured beads. It is also integral to more abstract concepts such as understanding numbers; take this sequence:

●, ●●, _____ , ●●●●, what is the missing element? We deduce it is three circles.

In this sequence 🕐,🕑,🕒,🕓, _____ the next clock will show half past six, and we can also work out earlier steps in the series. Developing the capacity to perceive and arrange things in order, naturally feeds into our general understanding of order in everyday life.

Development of seriation

Seriation grows on the foundations developed in the first 24 months. Rhythmic banging with a tool is one behaviour that draws attention to patterns and through banging the child becomes aware of repeated action-sequences. Continuant capacity is an essential prerequisite for seriation, as the child is now noticing and remembering the order of moving several objects around.

The ability to place an object at a specific point, is also important; the child must understand that there is a space at the end of a row, it is not finished! He must be able to visually scan along a line of blocks and coordinate his eyes and the movement of his hands, in order to put the object down in the right place. Many children with movement disorders or learning difficulties find this a real challenge; they often need play activities targeted to practise their eye-hand coordination before they can progress to seriation activities.

Stage 1. Early seriation: Chaining

This is the ability to deliberately place objects close together to make a long chain. The child deliberately repeats the action of adding to a line, first one then another one; he is aware of the space and the direction he is working in. The chains can grow in any horizontal direction from left to right, or right to left, towards the child or away from him, as well as diagonal lines across the table.

At the early stage, the chains are continuous and the elements are touching, but gradually the child perceives a row of bricks with gaps in between them, as a sequence. A chain can be made from a mixture of objects such as cars, bricks, yogurt pots etc. but gradually the tendency to select all the same emerges; this overlaps with the separating stage of the capacity to sort.

Stage 2. Active seriation
2a: Alternating sequence of objects

This is the ability to create repeating patterns and it grows from the experiences of moving collections of objects in order. It starts with the ability to place objects consecutively in a row of containers. This can be the pegs in the wooden boat or one fir cone into each saucer lined up in a row. This requires a clear understanding of space, position and order, and extrapolating 'which one is next?'

The ability to create an alternating sequence grows gradually; in the beginning there may be little evidence of order when the child arranges objects in a row. He may repeat a movement and return to the container where he last picked up a piece, not yet remembering to alternate and look for the second collection. With experience, his ability to keep two sets in mind will emerge and he can continue a sequence of alternating pieces: block, stone, block, stone etc.

2b: Getting bigger or smaller in size using objects

Active expansive series involve the perception of differences in the size of objects, big and small and some in between; the child is able to select objects more or less in size order. This means he can now build a tower of three to four bricks; he understands that the biggest brick goes at the bottom and the smaller ones on top; there is still a bit of trial and error. He can also put together a small set of nesting cups, one inside the other; again, some trial and error is involved, but the activity is carried out with an understanding that size matters.

Stage 3: Mature series
3a: Creating repeating patterns

This is the ability to extrapolate a pattern from looking at a sequence, and be able to continue the series in this same pattern. The child is now working more or less independently.

The first stage is to continue a sequence with two elements such as two shapes, colours or sizes; the difficulty increases with the number of elements in the pattern. There is a significant leap from being able to continue a simple alternating pattern with two elements like (brick, lid) (brick, lid), to perceiving the repeat in a sequence with three elements: (brick, lid, cone) (brick, lid, cone). There is a helpful intermediate stage where two elements are arranged as one unit: (brick, lid with a cone inside) (brick, lid with a cone inside) etc.

The next critical development is when the child starts to generate his own pattern sequences, playing with colours and shapes to create repeating series.

3b: Organising into size order

Mature expansive series describe objects arranged in size order such as a tower of cubes in different sizes or rings stacked on a cone-shaped pole. The earliest series have three elements and in time, the constructions become taller and with more pieces.

Expansive series can also be represented in 2-D with a series of shapes cut out in card; these can be lined up or placed one on top of the other, decreasing in size. This is a late development and it happens around the time when the child can recognise simple drawn series and extrapolate the patterns from looking at them. The child's understanding of series moves on from observation of physical attributes such as size, to conceptual understanding; take for example the different stages in the growth of a plant, the building of a house or blowing up a balloon. The child now has the capacity to make inferences about the past and the future from the fragments of the series available to him.

Teaching techniques

General set-up

Seriation is taught as part of the structured lesson and is introduced when the child can confidently choose and move objects around. It is grounded in the ability of 'putting in and taking out', which grows into placing objects with care and purpose.

- The facilitator builds the series with the child, guiding his hands as she creates the pattern; the actual sequences grow out of the repeated movements and this rhythmic placing should be really strong at the early stages.
- Create long lines and aim for the child to continue on his own.
- When the child is working unsupported, he may revert to simple lining up without including the two elements. The facilitator has to make a judgement, either:
    a) This is too advanced for the child at the moment, or
    b) Given support to instil the rhythmic picking up, he will be able to do it.
- Monitor the child's movement patterns carefully, and either return to simple putting in and exploring space or increase the support to establish alternating picking up and placing in a line.
- Sometimes a child decides to change a sequence, because he has noticed something new. This is the time to take charge and get the sequence back on track. The non-verbal message to the child is that 'This is the game we are playing now'. When he is playing by himself, he can explore his own series.

Equipment

Repeating series can be built with most objects that have a stable base such as bricks, corks, cylinders, bottle tops etc.; avoid objects that roll, they can cause frustration. It is useful to have some objects which stack on top of each other, as for example a bottle top on a brick or a cork in a jam-jar lid.

Expansive series can be built with stacking cups or boxes, Russian dolls or a cone-shaped stand with graded rings. It is also useful to have of set of bricks all the same size as they are ideal for building a staircase as this is another way of showing an expansive series. At the higher levels, homemade sequencing cards can be used to create interesting challenges and examples of these will follow in the section on mature seriation.

A sequencing board is a simple strip of wood or heavy cardboard which has been divided into identical squares, with eight to 10 spaces; it is used to organise a series of pictures.

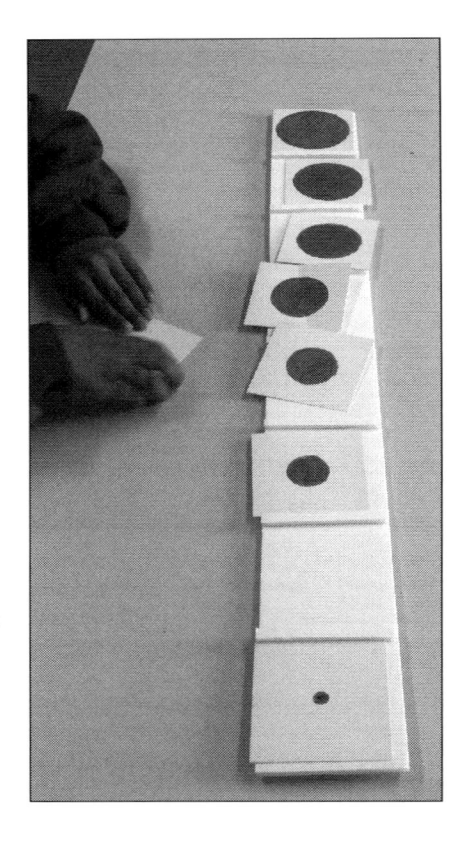

ACTIVITIES

STAGE 1. EARLY SERIATION
Chaining

These activities involve building long chains, working in different directions on the table. Initially the objects touch each other, later lines are created with a small space between the pieces. It is important to play these games slowly and to encourage the child to scan along the row before he puts his piece down; guide his hand with his pointing finger along the row all the way to the end, indicating 'the next space is at the end of the chain'.

All on-board

EQUIPMENT: Wooden boat and pegs.

ACTIVITY: The aim is to fill up the boat in order.

Step 1. Place the empty boat on the table.

Step 2. Present a peg, and point to the first hole in the boat. Support with hand over hand if necessary, to ensure the child gets it right.

Step 3. Pass the child one piece at a time, point to the next hole in the line; fade the pointing prompt when the child can continue on his own.

Step 4. Remove the pegs, one at a time, from one end to the other.

VARIATIONS: **a.** Fill the boat from right to left, giving the child one peg at a time.

b. Place the top half of the boat on the table. Move the pieces consecutively from one boat to the other, ensuring they are picked up in order and also placed in order.

c. Position the boats diagonally on the table and practise working right to left and left to right, continuing to pay attention to the order.

d. Place one empty boat upside down; remove one peg at a time from the full boat and line them up on top of the boat.

Making chains on a board

EQUIPMENT: Bricks, sequencing board or long strip of card.

ACTIVITY: The aim is to make a row without having a hole or grid to define the space.

Step 1. Place the sequencing board upside down so there are no dividers.

Step 2. Pass one brick at a time and support the child to make one long row on the board.

VARIATIONS: **a.** Build chains from right to left.

b. Turn the board 90°, this means working away from or towards himself.

c. Place the sequencing board the right way up, build a chain by placing one brick in each space. This activity introduces the idea that a row with gaps between the pieces is also a chain.

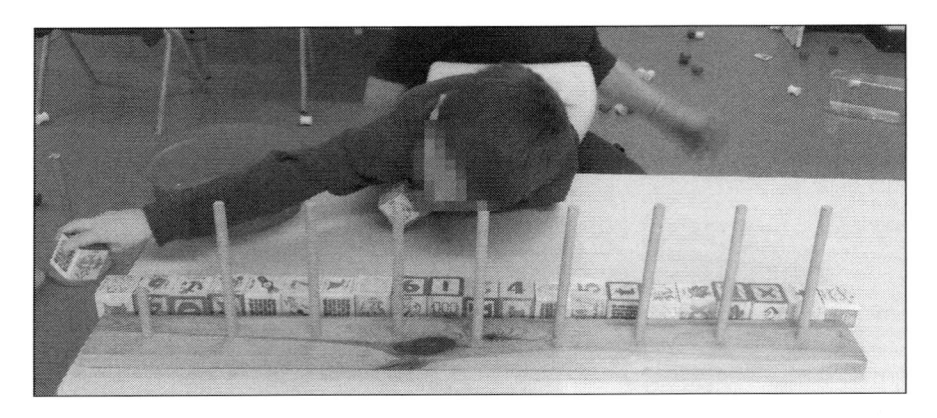

Build a chain without following a boundary

EQUIPMENT: Variety of small objects. Try to avoid objects that wobble or roll.

ACTIVITY: The aim is to create chains of objects on the table; the child should do this without support. Make sure the table has been cleared first.

Step 1. Present a tray full of objects. Start to line them up, creating a chain for the child to continue. Guide the child's hand to place an object next in the line.

Step 2. Reduce the support, first to a point, then aim for independence.

VARIATIONS:
a. Build chains in different directions.

b. Build chains that curve around corners or in a wavy line.

c. Practise adding to a row from both ends.

Show the child how to run his finger along the row to find the empty space at the end; this is the next space to be filled.

STAGE 2. ACTIVE SERIATION
2a. Alternating sequences

Alternating sequences can be created from many different elements e.g. two different objects, two different colours or shapes. The patterns can also be created with big and small blocks, big and small fir cones or two sizes of lolly sticks.

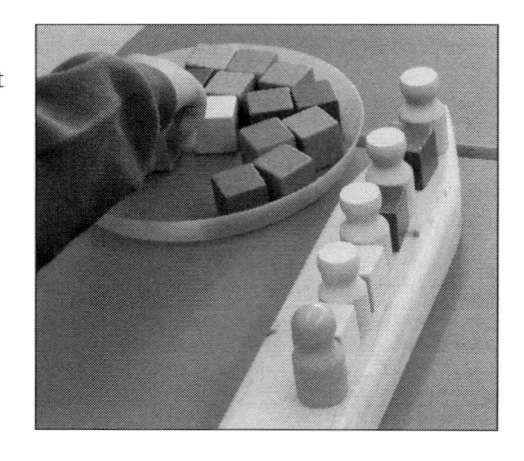

SECTION 3: PRACTICAL ACTIVITIES

Lots of rows

EQUIPMENT: Bricks, corks, cubes, lids.

ACTIVITY: The aim is to build lots of parallel rows.

Step 1. Start one row with the bricks. Encourage the child to continue on his own.

Step 2. Create a second row with different objects; the two chains run in parallel. Repeat with the other collections.

Step 3. The next stage is to dismantle the chains. Pick up all of one sort and put them into a box; repeat for every chain, ending up with all the pieces in their separate boxes.

VARIATION: The chains can be moved, piece by piece, to another part of the table.

Two rows become one

EQUIPMENT: Bricks and lids.

ACTIVITY: **Step 1.** Start by making a long chain of bricks, followed by arranging a second chain in front, this time made of lids.

Step 2. Move one lid at a time onto a brick; it is ok to have some lids left over.

Step 3. Separate this double chain into two boxes; first pick up one lid, then the brick, then a lid etc., always alternating between the two.

VARIATION: When taking the double chain apart, don't put the pieces in a box, instead create a new chain, but this time turning it into an alternating sequence.

Alternating sequence in the boat

EQUIPMENT: Boat, pegs and corks.

ACTIVITY: Place the two empty boat halves in extension of each other and the pegs and corks in separate trays.

Step 1. Give the child one object at a time, alternating pegs and corks.

Step 2. Provide guidance by pointing to the next hole in the boat, to help the child notice the order.

Step 3. Once finished, separate the chain into the two sets, working in order.

VARIATION: Use different materials which fit into the holes in the boat, such as small spatulas, bobbins or clothes pegs.

Can the child dismantle an alternating pattern in order?

Make an alternating sequence

EQUIPMENT: Boat with pegs, cotton reels.

ACTIVITY: This activity involves separating the objects into the two boats, then creating an alternating pattern on the table.

Step 1. Place the two halves of the empty boat on the table.
Fill up the first boat with pegs, then the second with cotton reels.

Step 2. Start to make an alternating pattern, guiding the child to pick up a peg and place it on the table, followed by a cotton reel from the second boat. Keep repeating this action until all the pieces are used and an alternating series has been created.

Step 3. Reverse the process, returning the pegs and cotton reels to their separate boats.

VARIATION: Give the child a box with the two different sorts all mixed together; separate these into the two boats followed by making an alternating sequence.

Many alternating sequences

EQUIPMENT: Wooden boat, bricks, cylinders, Unifix, rings, wooden discs.

ACTIVITY: The aim is for the child to continue the sequences unsupported.

Place the boats, upside-down, in extension of each other so they become a wall to build along. Choose two sets of objects to make the pattern.

Step 1. Start the sequence and guide the child to continue, 'first one of these then one of those'! If the child reverts to using just one element, help him to see the pattern by pointing to the next one in the series or guide his hands.

Step 2. Take the series apart, one piece at a time, separating the elements into trays.

VARIATIONS: **a.** Use a tool when the sequence is taken apart; pick up the cork, put it on the spoon, transfer it to the jug etc.

b. Focus on different characteristics:

- ▶ Colour: red/yellow/red/yellow; green/black/green/black etc.
- ▶ Shape: circle/triangle/circle/triangle; diamond/rectangle/diamond/rectangle etc.
- ▶ Size: long/short/long/short; big/small/big/small etc.
- ▶ Texture: rough/smooth/rough/smooth; soft/hard/soft/hard.

c. Place the two containers out of the direct field of vision; the child has to look around and reach out in order to collect the next piece.

STAGE 2. ACTIVE SERIATION
2a. Getting bigger or smaller

The expansive series can be created by building towers of bricks in different sizes as well as fitting nesting cups inside each other. This shows the emergence of understanding differences in size.

From big to small

EQUIPMENT: Graded stacking rings on a cone-shaped stand.

ACTIVITY: This stacking toy has an element of self-correction as the rings fit onto the cone in a set order. The child should explore this toy freely, putting the rings on and taking them off. He will not be setting out with the intention to learn about the size order of the rings, he simply enjoys playing and moving the rings about; he will gradually become aware of differences in size, how one ring slips on easily but the next one cannot fit on, there is a ring in the way! It is not important to complete this activity to make a perfectly arranged cone, instead give the child time and room for experimentation.

VARIATIONS: **a.** Use a kitchen roll stand instead of the cone-shaped stand. Let the child experiment with stacking the rings of different sizes on this stand, in any order he likes.

b. Russian dolls, no more than 5. Open up and take the doll out, put the two halves together again before opening the next one. The dolls can be arranged in height order.

Building up

EQUIPMENT: Five bricks in different sizes.

ACTIVITY: The aim is to help the child notice that this set of bricks can be stacked to create a stable tower. Please note, it is important to dismantle the tower every time and spread the bricks on the table before rebuilding.

Step 1. Start with three bricks in different sizes. Guide the hands to build a tower with three bricks, then quickly dismantle it.

Step 2. Next time, demonstrate building a tower and dismantle it. Now give the child the bricks and encourage him to rebuild it.

Step 3. Introduce a fourth brick, and repeat the activity above: model for the child, then it is his turn to build.

VARIATIONS: **a.** With three bricks in different sizes, model building up starting with the smallest. Will it balance or fall?

b. Try the activity with empty boxes, upside down nesting cups or cylinders.

c. Use a mixture of objects in different sizes - boxes, nesting cups, bottle tops and create a cone-like structure.

Do not play 'knocking down the tower'; the focus is on the emerging understanding that size and order really matters.

SECTION 3: PRACTICAL ACTIVITIES

Building along – getting bigger or smaller

EQUIPMENT: Set of five graded blocks.

ACTIVITY: **Step 1.** Start by building a tower of five blocks as described above.

Step 2. Remove the blocks, one at a time, and recreate the series horizontally on the table.

VARIATIONS: **a.** Move the series to somewhere else; this time start with the smallest and finish with the biggest.

b. When the series is built horizontally, emphasize the expanding nature of the sequence by placing a second object on each block, thus building up as well as along.

STAGE 3. MATURE SERIATION
3a. Creating repeating patterns

The critical development at this stage is the child's awareness of patterns; he understands that he is actively creating patterns and he can make both repeating sequences and series ordered according to size.

Series can also be represented in 2-D, which means working flat by ordering or stacking pieces of card in size order as well as exploring repeating patterns through drawing activities, such as colouring in or filling in the gaps.

Longer sequences, 2+1

EQUIPMENT: Bricks, rings, small cubes.

ACTIVITY: The aim is to understand a pattern with two or more elements; this is practised by combining two elements into one unit, hence the name 2+1.

Step 1. Start with a brick and place a small cube on top; next to this unit, place the ring.

Step 2. Repeat this pattern several times; step back to let the child continue without help when he appears confident to do so.

Step 3. Take the sequence apart, one piece at a time.

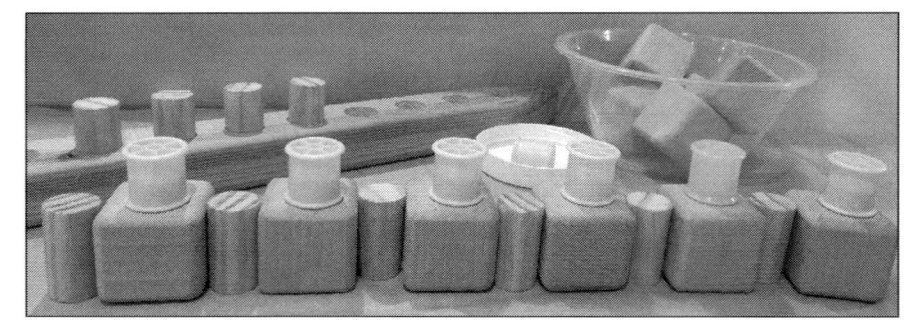

VARIATION: Practise 2+1 sequences with different objects; think of units such as a ring with a cone inside, a lid with a cube, a bottle top with a cork inside etc.

Sequences with three elements

EQUIPMENT: Bricks in three colours and three trays.

ACTIVITY: This game starts by separating the coloured bricks onto three trays and these colours are the basis for the repeating pattern.

Step 1. Put the three sorting trays on the table and seed each with a coloured brick. Give the child the box of bricks and demonstrate how to separate the colours; he is now ready to start the sequence.

Step 2. Start building a sequence, repeating the three colours; next involve the child, indicating that he should continue the pattern. Withdraw the help when the child understands what comes next in the line.

Step 3. Take the series apart, one brick at a time, returning the bricks to their original colour sets.

VARIATIONS: Use different collections of objects to create sequences:

- ▶ Coloured discs or cotton reels.
- ▶ Different shapes.
- ▶ Lolly sticks in different lengths.
- ▶ Large and small cubes or cylinders.

When the child makes a mistake, give him time to notice; what does he do next?

Create my own patterns

EQUIPMENT: Two identical sets of coloured bricks, presented in separate trays.

ACTIVITY: The aim is for the child to devise his own patterns. It starts with the adult leading the game, then the child is encouraged to devise his own pattern for the adult to copy. The adult and the child sit side by side with their separate sets of identical bricks.

Step 1. The adult starts an alternating sequence with two colours. The child copies, initially brick by brick, until he has internalised the pattern.
This series is then dismantled and the game is repeated with a new pattern.

Step 2. The adult signals to the child that it is his turn to start and the adult copies the pattern he makes, piece by piece, as it grows.

Step 3. Let the child take the lead to create sequences, using as many different elements as he wishes. The adult copies the child.

Patterns with three or more elements

EQUIPMENT: Mixture of bricks, corks, rings, shapes, different coloured lids etc.

ACTIVITY: The aim is for the child to understand the sequence and to continue in the same pattern on his own. If help is needed, this is best given with a point, 'Get one of those and place it there!' An upside-down H-board or the two halves of the boat, provide a clear edge to work along when lining up the sequence.

Step 1. Start a pattern with three elements and indicate to the child to continue this to make a long chain.

Step 2. Take the sequence apart, one piece at a time.

VARIATIONS: **a.** Increase the repeat in the pattern to four elements, first by using the +1 concept. The sequence can look something like this: (red bobbin, key, brick with a button on top) (red bobbin, key, brick with a button on top) etc.

b. Set up longer series and incorporate various elements into the repeat: different objects, colours, shapes and sizes.

c. Make sequences with four elements, but include two identical elements in the repeat; for example, (bobbin, shell, shell, brick) (bobbin, shell, shell, brick) etc.

d. Thread beads onto a string in a repeating pattern.

e. Use a kitchen roll stand and rings in three colours to make a vertical sequence.

f. Coloured clothes pegs placed in a colour sequence round the edge of a tray.

g. On completing a pattern, all the pieces can be gathered into one tray, then sorted.

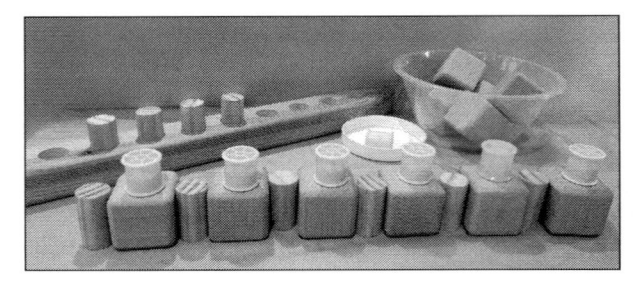

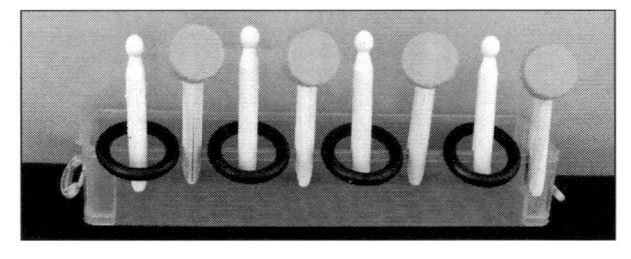

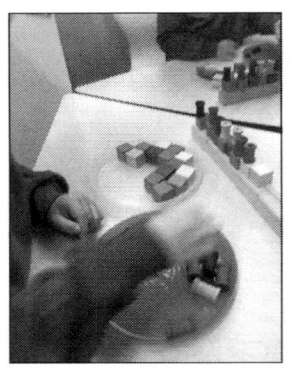

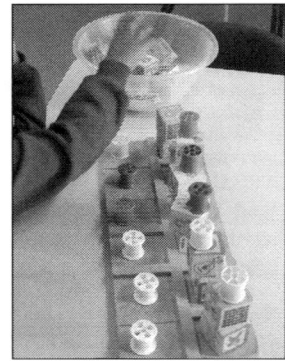

SECTION 3: PRACTICAL ACTIVITIES

Drawing repeating series

EQUIPMENT: Paper and pencil.

ACTIVITY: When the child is confident about colouring and drawing simple patterns, it is possible to create many different exercises to deepen his understanding of sequencing. Sit next to each other, and the adult draws a sequence whilst the child watches; she then passes the pen and paper to the child and he continues the pattern.

EXAMPLES:
a. Shape patterns: (circle, square, cross) (circle, square, cross) _ _ _ _ _ _

b. Colour patterns: (red, green, blue, yellow) (red, green, blue, yellow) _ _ _ _

c. Draw a line of boxes, position a ball: (in, on, under) (in, on, under) _ _ _ _ _

d. Directional clues like: (← ↑ → ↓) (← ↑ → ↓) _ _ _ _ _

Filling the gaps in a pattern

EQUIPMENT: Paper and pencil.

ACTIVITY: The aim is to understand the pattern from looking at a fragment of the whole; for example, what is missing in this sequence: red, green, blue, red, green, blue, ___ , green, blue, ___ etc. The child fills in the gaps.

EXAMPLES:
a. O O X Y O O _ Y O O X _ O O

b. (⌒) ⌣ (_) ⌣ _

c. _ • ● ○ ◉ • ● _ ◉ • ● ○ _

3b. Organising into order of size

Build a staircase

EQUIPMENT: Uniform collection of bricks.

ACTIVITY: The aim is to build a staircase pattern of bricks.

Step 1. Make a row of six or seven bricks.

Step 2. Go back to the beginning, indicate to start the second layer on the second brick, continue to the end.

Step 3. Decrease each layer by one brick until the staircase is complete.

VARIATIONS:
a. Place an extra object on each step on the staircase; this helps to draw attention to the expanding nature of the structure.

b. Create a similar pattern, this time lying it flat on the table.

c. Build a roof-shaped structure. Make a line of seven bricks, the next layer has five starting on the second brick, third layer has three bricks, finishing with one at the top.

SECTION 3: PRACTICAL ACTIVITIES

An expansive series can be lying down!

EQUIPMENT: Blocks in different sizes, square rods or cylinders in different lengths.

ACTIVITY: The focus is on understanding that an expansive series can be built lying flat on the table; they do not have to be built up nor stand up.

Step 1. With a set of blocks in different sizes, build them up into a tower.

Step 2. Dismantle the tower piece by piece and arrange them on the table in a long line.

Step 3. Repeat this exercise but leave out the first step of building up; this time start with the smallest and finish with the largest, arranging the blocks in size order.

VARIATIONS: **a.** Explore different forms such as graded nesting cups or cardboard tubes cut into different lengths.

b. Use a mixed set such as a chop stick, a drinking straw, a lolly-stick and a tooth pick and arrange these in order of length.

c. When arranging a series of graded forms, intersperse them with other objects; this expands the sequence.

Noticing order everywhere!

EQUIPMENT: Cards with drawn series; seriation board.

ACTIVITY: Picture cards can be used to create wide-ranging learning experiences of repeating patterns, various expansive series and advanced concepts of how things expand or change over time.

Start the series by placing the first card on the board, spread the remaining cards around. Give the child sufficient support to carry out the activity, whilst always allowing him to make his own decisions.

EXAMPLES: **a.** Series of six to eight pictures of squares or circles, decreasing in size.

b. Cards showing increasing quantities e.g. one, a few, several, lots of balls.

c. Changes in shade from light to dark.

d. Steps in blowing up a balloon, getting bigger and bigger.

e. Flagpole with a flag being raised, step by step to the top.

f. Flying a kite, on each card the kite is higher/smaller.

g. A plant growing out of the ground, step by step, showing how it matures.

h. A car on a racing track, getting closer and closer to the finishing line.

Here are some examples of sequencing cards. The first two relate to changes in size, the third is an expansive series relating to the concept of quantity. The last two examples are conceptual, understanding how things can change over time.

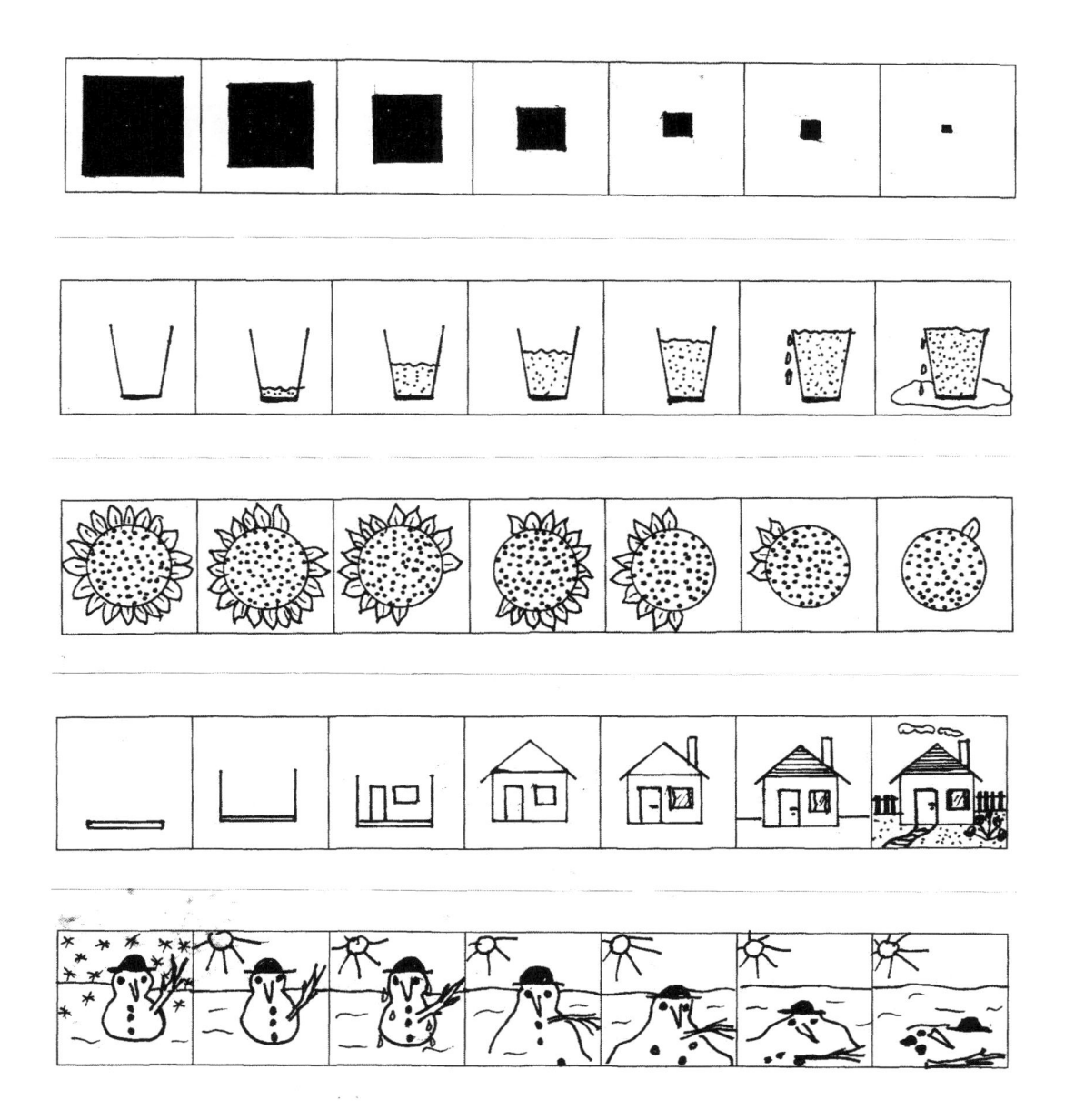

SECTION 3: PRACTICAL ACTIVITIES

DRAWING

Definition

Drawing is defined as the capacity to hold a tool in the hand and to make marks with it. This grows into the ability to draw shapes and pictures as well as copy patterns.

Links

Drawing is clearly linked to tool-use; it is a special case of using a tool, this one will make marks on the surface. Drawing also has links to brick-building which is concerned with representing the world in three dimensions, whereas drawing is the understanding of space in two dimensions; both capacities involve understanding the positions of objects and how these relate to each other. One of the early matching skills is to make pairs of simple geometric shapes such as two circles, crosses or squares; the child can match these patterns a long time before he is able to copy or draw them.

Development of drawing

Drawing originates from the large movements of the arms from the shoulder and developing an awareness of the space the arms can occupy. Holding the pen in the hand develops from the ability to grip a toy and use it to bang and scrape against surfaces, often in a rhythmic pattern. The child discovers what happens when he strikes a spoon against the table: it makes a noise or leaves a trail in the crumbs. Later he starts to notice the marks being left behind by the crayon in his hand or the stick in the sand. That is the beginning of deliberate mark-making.

Stage 1. Early drawing: Making a mark

The first stage is called deliberate mark-making; with a stick or a crayon in his hand, the child makes large movements which become banging and scraping motions. He notices and pays attention to the marks left behind when he repeatedly taps with a crayon on a surface.

Stage 2. Active drawing: Drawing lines

The next developmental stage is to draw lines and initially this happens when the child moves his hands back and forth in front of himself. He also starts to scribble in a continuous circular pattern, akin to the stirring of a pot. He discovers how to deliberately stop and start a line by lifting the pencil off the page – this is an important discovery. He begins to explore the lines, and he reaches out and across to draw lines towards himself.

The next stage is being able to pay attention when someone else is drawing; the child will be influenced by the drawings of someone sitting next to him. He may change the direction of his scribbling but he is still far from able to copy a drawing. A child at this stage will watch an adult draw a cross and his own response is likely to be two parallel lines, not crossing!

Stage 3. Mature drawing: Drawing shapes and pictures

The child has now reached a stage where he can stop and start lines and draw them in different directions. He can attend to how the lines are linked such as crossing over or meeting in a corner. This means the child is starting to analyse how a shape is constructed which will lead to the ability to copy, i.e. he understands a square is a shape made from four lines and has four corners. He starts to attend to the relative proportions of the elements and their position within a figure. Take, for example, a car, it is essentially a rectangle and two circles: the wheel shapes are placed roughly in the correct positions and drawn approximately to the right size.

At this stage children vary greatly in their ability to copy a drawing and this is naturally influenced by their previous experiences; some children spend lots of time drawing, others do not. The child can now look at a drawing and begin to understand how it is constructed and recognise the separate elements within it, but his understanding is very different from the adult's. When it comes to copying a model drawn by an adult, the child's interpretation is likely to look very different from the original!

Teaching techniques

General set-up

Drawing is taught as part of the structured learning session; it follows on naturally from rhythmic banging and scraping activities. Many children are often inhibited when they are introduced to banging and scraping so the adult must take the lead and convey the feeling of fun and enjoyment; this is a great way to explore. The child should experience a strong rhythm and a great variety of movements and actions. It can be noisy, so plan this activity with consideration so it doesn't disturb others. The facilitator should sit behind the child during the practice of early drawing. The focus at the early stages is to:

- Be effortful and persevere.
- Encourage large body movements and rhythmic patterns.
- Practise firm control of the crayon.
- Move on from making marks to drawing lines.
- Draw lines in many different directions.
- Finish lines in different places on the paper.
- Begin to create patterns by making sharp changes of direction.

As the child reaches the mature drawing stage, it is recommended to sit side by side so the child can watch the adult draw and enjoy the turn-taking games.

Equipment

- It is useful to have two heavy wooden hammers, drum sticks or large wooden spoons.
- Use good quality paper, minimum A3 size; masking tape is great for fixing the paper to the table, preventing it from sliding around.
- Crayons are generally better than felt-tip pens, they require firmer pressure and the child has to put in more effort. Felt-tip pens can easily split; banging these create a splatter effect and that behaviour can become a real a distraction.
- Include a variety of drawing media such as large pencils, finger crayons, paint, graphite, sand and glue etc.

The focus is always on the experience and not the final picture.

SECTION 3: PRACTICAL ACTIVITIES

DRAWING ACTIVITIES

STAGE 1. EARLY DRAWING
Making a mark

Rhythmic banging and scraping

EQUIPMENT: Two wooden sticks and objects to strike e.g. a metal tin, carboard box or washing up bowl.

ACTIVITY: This activity is also described in chapter 7 under Tool use.

Sit behind the child and support him to hold a substantial stick or hammer in each hand.

Step 1. Create a rhythm, arms up and down, and banging down on the table.

Step 2. Explore different patterns of rhythmic banging:

- Hard and gentle.
- Fast and slow.
- Banging with one stick, then the other.
- Both arms moving together in unison, then alternating the left and right arm.

Step 3. Make scraping movements with the sticks:

- Side to side.
- Towards and away from the body.
- Circling around on the table.
- Practise the patterns first with one hand, then both hands together.
- Incorporate changes in direction, left to right, right to left.

VARIATIONS: **a.** Place a washing up bowl upside down on the table; use it as a drum and create different drumming patterns.

b. Move the bowl from side to side by hitting it, to and fro.

c. Explore the different sounds the sticks can make by hitting the table, the washing up bowl, the table legs, the chair; try all the different surfaces within reach.

d. Place several containers made from different materials on the table and explore the variety of sounds that can be made by banging these; keep the emphasis on a strong rhythm.

Xylophone and chime bars

EQUIPMENT: Xylophone or chime bars, beaters.

ACTIVITY: The activity is a variation on the rhythmic banging described above, using a small xylophone or a set of chime bars. The aim is to explore the movements of reaching out and hitting the notes, playing different rhythmic patterns, changing the speed and the force with which the notes are struck. The child may need the adult support at first, but gradually reduce the help given and let him continue on his own.

Making marks

EQUIPMENT: Large piece of paper, masking tape and jumbo crayons.

ACTIVITY: In preparation, tape a large piece of paper to the table.

Step 1. Support the child to hold the crayon in one hand. Make tapping marks by lifting and dropping the hand down so it hits the paper and leaves a mark; repeat this action many times over.

Step 2. Continue to create marks in different parts of the paper; tap down, stop and look, then make a few more. Cover the paper in simple marks.

VARIATIONS: **a.** Swap the crayon from one hand to the other, ensuring that both the left and the right hand practise the movements.

b. Make marks by holding a crayon in both hands at the same time.

c. Change the colours and change the type of crayons used.

SECTION 3: PRACTICAL ACTIVITIES

STAGE 2. ACTIVE DRAWING
Drawing lines

At this stage the child starts to scribble and draw lines; he also makes continuous, circular patterns. Next, he discovers how to stop and start a line by lifting the pencil off the page. He begins to attend to other people's drawings and respond to those in his own way.

Drawing lines in the sand

EQUIPMENT: Sand tray, short sticks.

ACTIVITY: **Step 1.** Sit or stand by the sand tray. With guidance, draw lines with a finger in the sand - up and down, left to right, straight and circular scribbles.

Step 2. Smooth over the surface and start again. Keep going until the child gets fully engrossed and he continues to make patterns on his own.

VARIATIONS: **a.** Use both hands to draw with, one finger or several; explore variations of straight and curvy lines.

b. Make lines and patterns with a stick.

c. Use a tray with different play material to draw in such as oats, cornflour, wood shavings etc.

Drawing lines

EQUIPMENT: Paper and crayons.

ACTIVITY: This activity transfers the movement patterns explored in the sand, to paper. Secure the paper to the table with masking tape.

Step 1. To introduce the activity, help the child to hold a crayon in each hand and guide his movements, explore:

- ▶ Strong lines from top to bottom.
- ▶ Side to side.
- ▶ Circular movements in opposite directions.
- ▶ First one hand, then the other or both hands together.

SECTION 3: PRACTICAL ACTIVITIES

Step 2. Fade the physical support to encourage the child to continue making lines on the paper by himself.

VARIATIONS: **a.** Change the size of the paper and thereby also the size of the movements needed to fill the paper; work big and work small.

b. Change the colour of the crayons.

c. Draw with different sorts of crayons and coloured pencils.

d. Draw a line and make a definite stop; lift the crayon, take a look, before making another line somewhere else on the paper. Cover the paper in ever changing lines.

Start at the dot!

EQUIPMENT: Paper and crayons.

ACTIVITY: The aim is to focus on one point and understand this is where the line starts.

Step 1. The adult holds a crayon in one hand and supports the child's hand with the other, holding a crayon together. The adult draws a big dot at the top of the page; next, support the child to stretch out and draw a line from this dot, all the way down the page towards himself.

Step 2. Repeat drawing dot after dot at the top of the page, gradually filling the page with lines. Reduce the help given to the child.

VARIATIONS: **a.** Draw a row of dots along the side of the paper; practise drawing from left to right. Reverse, this time drawing from right to left.

b. Practise all the above variations with both hands.

Is the child looking at and tracking his hand as he draws a line?

Beginning to copy lines

EQUIPMENT: Large piece of paper and crayons.

ACTIVITY: Fold the paper in half and draw a line down the middle. The adult will draw lines on one half and the aim is for the child to copy on his half of the page. The adult might need to guide the child's drawing hand when the activity is introduced.

Step 1. Slowly and deliberately draw a line from the top to the bottom, followed immediately by supporting the child to do the same.

Step 2. Repeat the routine, alternating between the adult drawing a line followed by the child doing the same.

Step 3. Reduce the physical prompt when the child starts to draw the lines by himself.

Please note: at this stage the turn-taking aspect is an important part of the activity; it provides an opportunity for the child to switch his attention between watching the adult draw and learning to copy her actions.

VARIATIONS: **a.** The child and the adult use different coloured crayons.

b. Build in a routine of changing the crayon after each line which creates a colourful drawing of vertical stripes.

Copying the lines in different directions

EQUIPMENT: Large piece of paper with a dividing line down the centre; crayons.

ACTIVITY: The set-up is the same as for the activity above: both the child and the adult has a crayon, each drawing on their side of the paper.

Step 1. First the adult draws a line, then it is the child's turn to copy. The lines can be drawn in different directions on the page, from top to bottom, corner to corner etc. Guide the child to the right point on the page before he starts his lines.

Step 2. Vary the starting points, use the corners, start on the left side or the right side, top or bottom, and continue to fill the page.

VARIATIONS: **a.** Introduce curved lines.

b. Draw lines with a sharp change in direction such as V and L shapes.

STAGE 3. MATURE DRAWING
Drawing shapes and pictures

At this stage the child should hold the pencil and complete the tasks independently. Make sure he steadies the paper with one hand as the whole body is involved in the actions of drawing and writing.

Games can be prepared in advance, targeting the abilities to scan a page, to locate the starting and finishing points, as well as practising the skill of using a pencil.

The general technique for joining up games can be broken down into a sequence of steps:

- ▶ Point out where to start the line.
- ▶ With the other hand, point to the finishing spot.
- ▶ Run the finger up and down from the start to finish, then draw!

However, not every step is necessary for all children. Be flexible and adapt the approach to encourage independence.

Joining the dots

EQUIPMENT: Paper marked with 8 dots, scattered around the page; crayons.

ACTIVITY: Each of the dots can be seen as either a starting or a finishing point.

Step 1. The adult runs her finger from one dot to another; next guide the child to draw a line between them.

Step 2. Continue to join the dots in pairs.

VARIATIONS: **a.** Join each dot to several others, creating a criss-cross pattern.

b. Start with 10 or more dots on the page.

c. Repeat the exercise with different coloured crayons.

d. Mark a small circle in the centre of the page, with lots of dots scattered around the edges; the lines are drawn from the centre out and create a star.

Join the shapes

EQUIPMENT: Paper and pencil.

ACTIVITY: In preparation, draw a number of shapes along the left side of the paper, repeat these in a different order on the right; these are to be joined up in pairs.

It requires a high level of understanding to match and join shapes on the page as the child has to look at the two sets of shapes and locate the pairs, then join them up.

Start with just a few shapes. Draw the line between the shapes with the finger before using the pencil; gradually introduce a greater number of shapes. There is great value in repeating exercises with variations before adding to the complexity.

VARIATIONS: There are many variations of 'Join the shapes' game:

- Join the shapes from left to right and right to left.
- Draw the shapes at the top and the bottom of the page.
- Draw the pairs of shapes randomly on the page.
- Draw similar but not identical shapes to be joined.
- Join coloured dots.
- Join other graphic patterns such as ◉, ⌃, ༄, ⊠, �, ×, ✶.
- Join letter shapes.

Copying shapes

EQUIPMENT: Paper and pencil.

ACTIVITY: The aim is for the child to copy a shape drawn by the adult.

Divide the paper into two rectangles, one for the child and one for the adult to draw on. After drawing a shape, guide the child to do the same but reduce the help when he knows what to do. His drawing will not be a perfect copy, it will be an interpretation which reflects his current level of understanding.

Step 1. The adult draws a simple shape such as a circle; the child looks at the model and makes an attempt to copy.

Step 2. Repeat with other simple shapes such as two parallel lines; a triangle; a cross drawn in two stages, which means the child copies line by line.

VARIATIONS: **a.** Reverse the roles and the child leads; it is time for the adult to follow.

b. Build up a picture by drawing several different shapes e.g. a square and a triangle to make a house.

SECTION 3: PRACTICAL ACTIVITIES

Writing practice

EQUIPMENT: Paper and pencil.

ACTIVITY: There are many different patterns and exercises designed to promote the skills of drawing and writing. These generally focus on a specific outcome as supposed to the general abilities and understanding. However, there is still merit in spending time practising the pencil skills as they are transferable skills. Here are some familiar activities:

- Trace along dotted lines.
- Draw between lines.
- Copy a row of shapes.
- On a 3x3 grid, draw a shape in each square.
- Colour in shapes.
- Trace around shapes.

Create patterns with shapes and draw them

EQUIPMENT: Straws or small lolly sticks, other flat shapes; paper and pencil.

ACTIVITY: The aim is to create shapes from different materials, then represent these on the paper.

Step 1. Lay out the lolly sticks to create a shape, for example a star, a square or a triangle.

Step 2. Draw round this shape.

Step 3. Copy the shape instead of drawing round it.

VARIATIONS:
a. Trace around flat shapes such as circles, oblongs, triangles, squares etc.

b. Feel the shape in one hand and draw it with the other.

c. Create figures combining several shapes and then copy these on paper.

BRICK-BUILDING

Definition

This learning to learn capacity encompasses the ability to analyse the spatial relationships between objects and leads to the understanding of how to create and copy 3-dimensional structures.
In essence, it is the ability to create models and also to build a model by following a plan or an illustration.

The beginning of brick-building is making piles of objects in all different shapes and sizes. The child experiences what happens when he piles things up: one piece might balance or fit into a hole, another rolls down or settles in a gap. Out of these experiences emerge the interest and the ability to deliberately create structures, and the growing understanding of the variety of shapes and their position in relation to each other. I have chosen to use the commonly accepted word shape when referring to a 3-dimensional form.

Take a look at this seemingly simple bridge structure of four pieces. First the child must identify the individual pieces, then he has to analyse their relative positions and their orientation, and also understand that the gap between the pieces can be bridged with a single block. Putting all this information together shows an advanced ability to analyse and translate ideas from a 2-dimensional picture into a 3-dimensional model.

Some children with learning difficulties do not progress to the higher levels of understanding 3-dimensional spatial relationships and sometimes they get stuck in repetitive and obsessional play habits. They may repeat an activity over and over, such as building a tower and knocking it down or meticulously lining up the bricks in one way only, their way! Such repetitive routines provide hardly any new experiences from which to learn, as variations are essential. The child needs to explore and learn to tolerate unexpected events such as piling up lots of materials and watching what happens next.

Links

Brick-building grows out of the early bodily integration: the understanding of spatial relationships starts with understanding movements in relation to oneself, the abilities to confidently move the arms and use the hands. Other learning to learn capacities like matching and seriation, are integral to brick-building; it is clear that a child needs the ability to match two shapes before he can attempt to copy a model; he must also identify a shape from a drawing in order to build it. Seriation is also important, both repeating patterns and the understanding of expansive series which are concerned with the relative sizes, big and small, long and short, equal size etc.

Everyday brick-building

So many everyday tasks rely on our ability to understand 3-dimensional space though we are rarely consciously aware of it. For example, how to fit the food and drink into the lunch box or tidy the toys away on the shelf; for the child who is building a den with boxes, chairs and a blanket or organising his cars and lorries in the play garage, onto quite another level: the adult who is designing furniture or the architect drawing plans for a sky-scraper; the brick-building capacity is used everywhere!

Development of brick-building

Stage 1. Early brick-building: Piling

The early stage of brick-building is piling and this is a very important activity. As the word implies, it entails making piles from a variety of bits and pieces, be it fir cones, sticks, bricks, lids, tubes, yogurt pots etc. All these materials will behave in different ways when they are piled up and the child will notice how some roll, some will balance, some will settle into gaps, some fit behind and others in front, sit on the top or lie by the side. Every pile is a new experience and it adds to the understanding of the objects and space; the child experiences how some structures are stable and others less so, some pieces do not settle and they slide off. Through countless experiences of building piles, his understanding grows as well as his tolerance to deal with the unexpected.

During the structured session, it is important to quickly dismantle the piles and make new ones; the piles are not finished structures to be kept, but the result of the ongoing play. Continue to explore the materials anew with yet another pile.

Stage 2. Active brick-building: Planning what to build

The child can now deliberately place the blocks and think about where each piece should go and he moves everything with purpose. His finished building is unlikely to resemble anything specific. The child will watch an adult engaged in a building activity, playing around with where and how to place the bricks; this might subsequently influence the child in how he develops his structure, maybe building up or along in the same way as the adult.

At this stage the child builds with an idea in mind, he may or may not verbalise his plan. The child has the intention to construct something specific and he is no longer simply making a pile. The completed model may not bear any resemblance to the stated plan and the idea for the building can indeed change along the way: for example, he may have planned a car but in the process of construction, it becomes a farm or a rocket; for the child this is completely normal.

Stage 3. Mature brick-building: Copying and building

The key development in mature brick-building is the ability to copy a model. Firstly, the child is able to identify differently shaped bricks and secondly, he is learning to copy a simple structure.

This requires the ability to examine the model and to analyse it systematically. The child must look at the whole and the individual parts, have a go at building and regularly check against the model. The skills include the recognition of bridging components, the orientation of all the elements, seeing the overall shapes and the hidden supporting elements; there are many layers of complexity which develop with age and experience.

The higher level of mature brick-building is the ability to construct models by following a step by step plan, and eventually, the child will be able to look at a drawing, analyse it in detail and reproduce the structure without a plan to follow.

Teaching techniques

Brick-building is practised during the structured session.

- ▶ Incorporate a lengthy session of piling; repeat the activity several times to create different experiences with the same collection of mixed materials.
- ▶ Initially the child benefits from hand over hand guidance to construct the pile, but gradually reduce the help, aiming for him to continue independently.
- ▶ In order to play at stage 2, active brick-building, the child must be able to attend to the adult's construction and handle the material by himself.
- ▶ During active brick-building, the child and the adult sit alongside each other; the adult creates various structures and takes them apart again. The child is not yet expected to copy but he should show an interest and be influenced by what he sees.
- ▶ At stage 3, mature brick-building, the child is expected to copy a given model.

Equipment

1. Piling material is a mixed collection of bits and pieces – tubes, lids, pegs, bricks, fir cones, conkers, everything used for picking up and putting in activities.

2. Mature building material consists of wooden building blocks in different shapes; these are available commercially. The bricks can be made in natural wood or painted in many colours; both sets are suitable though colour is not important for the activities.

BRICK-BUILDING ACTIVITIES

STAGE 1. EARLY BRICK-BUILDING
Piling

The activity involves making piles of mixed materials, some regular shapes like bricks, rings, beads, bobbins, cylinders, yogurt pots, empty boxes as well as more irregular shapes like screwed up paper, stones, feathers, sticks of different weight and length, or empty tins; even potatoes, carrots, leeks and onions are great for piling!

Let's fill the bowl

EQUIPMENT: One set of similar, but irregularly shaped pieces like a bag of potatoes.

A shallow bowl which allows the child to see what is inside.

ACTIVITY: Spread the objects around on the table and place the bowl in the centre.

Step 1. Pick up and 'dump' each piece into the bowl; this means discouraging the child from carefully arranging and fitting everything neatly together; he is simply piling it into the tray.

Step 2. Keep piling up, taking time to do so.

Step 3. When the bowl is getting full, the objects start to fall off; give the child time to pick them up and replace them. Observe him carefully and note how he reacts to the potential frustration of the wobbly pile. Once the pile is considered large enough, start again and refill the tray.

VARIATIONS:
a. Use a different bowl or tray to make the pile in; think about the size and shape which will create a new experience.

b. Choose another set of oddly shaped objects to make the pile.

Pile it all!

EQUIPMENT: Variety of objects.

One large shallow basket and a metal tray.

ACTIVITY: The aim is to build a 'bonfire' in one container, then rebuild it in another.

Step 1. Place the basket on the table, give the child one object at a time to add to the heap.

Step 2. Constantly vary the items to be added: a heavy stone, a long stick, a fir cone, a ping pong ball etc.

Step 3. Once the pile reaches the stage where nothing else will stay and it falls off, it is time to start all over again. Give the child the metal tray, and demonstrate how each piece can be moved from the basket and a new stack created in the tray.

VARIATIONS:
a. Spread a load of objects on the table; the child piles them all into the basket on his own.

b. Whilst the child is building his pile, the facilitator starts to join in; she adds pieces of her own, here and there, to change the structure a little bit.

Fruit and veg

EQUIPMENT: Tray.

Mixture of vegetables such as onions, carrots and potatoes.

ACTIVITY: Give the child one vegetable at a time to be added to the tray; the differently shaped vegetables create a new challenge of how to balance and fit everything together.

VARIATION: Keep the vegetables in their separate bags and as an extra step, the child has to remove them from the bags first, one at a time, and put them in the basket.

Fill the ring

EQUIPMENT: Piece of rope.

Mixed collection of objects.

ACTIVITY: Create a circular shape with the rope: this is to define the area where the 'bonfire' is to be built. This is a slow and deliberate exploration in stacking a collection of oddments, and the child will experience the constantly changing nature of the structure.

Step 1. Pass one object at a time to be placed on the stack. Let the child take time to place the pieces and to return them, if they fall off.

Step 2. Spread the material on the table and reshape the rope. Time to build another bonfire.

VARIATIONS: **a.** Create different shapes with the rope to work within such as a figure of eight, this means two piles side by side.

b. Give the child a basket full of stuff. He picks the pieces and makes a pile of his own choosing.

Can the child build a pile without help and can he manage his emotions if the pieces fall off?

STAGE 2. ACTIVE BRICK-BUILDING
Planning what to build

This is the beginning of model-making. The child can arrange the pieces without guidance and when he builds, he has an idea in his mind. He is influenced by other models he can see, but he is not yet at the stage of copying.

Making pairs of building blocks

EQUIPMENT: Pairs of wooden building blocks: cubes, cylinders, oblongs, triangles, semi-circles.

Two large saucers.

ACTIVITY: The purpose of this exercise is to establish that the child can match the pairs of different building blocks. The game is played as Pairing which is described in the chapter on matching.

Step 1. Two large saucers, one each for the child and the adult. Spread the pairs of matching blocks on the table. The adult picks up one block and guides the child to find the twin; the adult puts her block in her saucer and points to the child's saucer, indicating that he should place his block in there.

Step 2. Continue to pair up all the blocks, placing them in the separate trays.

Step 3. Play the game again to establish that the child can confidently find the matching pairs of blocks.

VARIATIONS: **a.** Start with the pairs separated into the two saucers. The adult holds up one of her blocks, the child locates the match in his tray. Both the blocks are returned to the separate sets; repeat in order to pair all the pieces.

b. Play pairing as a turn-taking game, first the adult shows a piece, and the child finds the match; then the child leads, he selects a block and the adult looks for the match.

Step by step building

EQUIPMENT: Two identical sets of building blocks.

ACTIVITY: The aim is for the child to copy the adult, placing one block at a time, to create a small structure. The child and the adult sit next to each other with the sets of matching blocks.

Step 1. The facilitator selects a block and places it on the table; she then indicates non-verbally to the child to do the same, using a point or a simple gesture.

Step 2. Pick up another block and place it on top; the child copies. Repeat with one or two more pieces, placing them by the side, on top or in front.

Step 3. Dismantle the structure one piece at a time, the child copying the adult step by step.

At this stage, ensure the child picks up the pieces in the same way and in the same order as the adult; the emphasis is on understanding the shapes and the movements.

VARIATIONS: **a.** Create buildings with three or four different blocks arranged in more unusual positions such as behind, underneath or an arch between two blocks.

b. Consider the wider range of orientations of the blocks; an oblong can lie down or stand on its end; a triangle can be placed in several ways; encourage close scrutiny of the model.

Let's build

EQUIPMENT: Set of wooden building blocks.

ACTIVITY: The aim is to provide the child with an opportunity to observe and notice how models are built; in this game he is not expected to copy step by step as in the previous game. First, he observes and then he creates his own building.

Step 1. Sit side by side. The adult builds a simple model, taking time to do so and giving the child plenty of time to observe.

Step 2. The child creates his own building. This may or may not be a copy of the adult's model.

Step 3. Dismantle both models and build something new.

VARIATION: When the child builds a model, pay attention to it and use some of his ideas in the next model.

Does the child pay attention to the adult's building and is he influenced by what he sees?

Taking turns to lead

EQUIPMENT: Wooden building blocks.

ACTIVITY: Sit side by side, each with identical sets of building blocks.

Step 1. The adult makes a simple 3/4-piece model and the child copies it. Quickly disassemble both buildings, ready to start again.

Step 2. Reverse the roles: it is now the child's turn to start. The adult copies his structure, slowly and carefully.

Step 3. Continue to take it in turns to build and to copy. Do not correct the child if he doesn't copy accurately, instead build a similar but slightly different model next time.

VARIATIONS: **a.** Increase the number of building blocks used; this allows for a wider range of models.

b. Introduce small anomalies such as not copying the model exactly. Wait for the child's response: does he notice? If yes, what does he do?

Children engaged in these activities will often comment or ask "My turn?" It is entirely appropriate to answer such questions, but keep the conversation to a minimum.

SECTION 3: PRACTICAL ACTIVITIES

Building with different materials

EQUIPMENT: Mixed collection of building materials like straws, cardboard tubes, buttons, empty boxes, jars etc.

ACTIVITY: Sit next to the child, with two similar collections of objects.

Step 1. Start to build a model; the child has to locate the same pieces in his tray and place them in the same way.

Step 2. Dismantle and create a different structure.

Step 3. The child takes the lead and the adult copies his model.

VARIATIONS: **a.** Sit side by side and build separate structures at the same time; these can become quite complex with many pieces added. Take time to pay attention to each other, and incorporate some of the child's ideas.

b. Keep all the material in one shared box, rummage to find what is needed to build.

STAGE 3. MATURE BRICK-BUILDING
Copying and building

At this stage the child is ready to copy a model; it is normal for children to make mirror images and this should be accepted but ensure that the rest is accurate. The aim of the activities is to increase the children's understanding of a structure and their ability to analyse it, not to teach them how to reproduce specific models.

The understanding of spatial relationships grows gradually through experience. There are some identifiable elements of 3-D construction which it is important to understand. However, the child's progression is not linear and his understanding will develop across the spectrum.

Brick-building can be played as a turn-taking activity: the adult makes a model, the child copies; take the models apart and start again, this time the child leads. There is no need to be rigid in the approach, instead be responsive to each other and have fun in building together.

It is useful to have a set of commercial building blocks as it is designed as a coherent whole with a variety of forms, sizes etc. However, similar experiences can easily be created with a collection of odd materials which is readily available like empty yogurt pots, lids, small boxes, lolly sticks, cardboard tubes etc. Take time to play together, explore and enjoy.

The following examples illustrate the increasing complexity of 3-dimensional models. The child's understanding of shape, space and spatial relationships will develop through different building experiences. The examples shown here are just the starting point for creating new models; the possibilities are endless.

Elements of construction	Examples
i. Simple models with blocks positioned in front, behind, beside and on top	
ii. Models with symmetrical components	
iii. Models with a number of different elements	
iv. Models with sub-structures or hidden elements	

SECTION 3: PRACTICAL ACTIVITIES

CODING

Definition

Coding is defined as the capacity to associate two signs or symbols in an arbitrary way so one comes to represent another. Take, for example, a triangle, this will have different meanings depending on the context.

- As a street sign, it is a warning triangle.
- It can also refer to the word spelled 'triangle'.
- In some contexts, this represents fire.
- On the washing instructions, it means 'bleach'.

There are two different strands of codes; the first relate to temporary associations between two symbols and the second, permanent codes, which have agreed and accepted meanings that people share. One obvious example of a permanent code is the spoken language: certain sounds have acquired an agreed meaning. When someone says the word 'cup', everyone understands it means an implement used to drink from. Writing is another example of a permanent code where the mix of shapes called letters are combined into strings and given meaning we can read and understand. Picture symbol systems are another way of attaching permanent meaning which have a shared understanding. However, symbols can also have temporary meanings. This is seen in algebra where the value of x is constantly changing, $x = 7.1$ in one equation but in another $x = 2$. The basis for both strands of codes is the understanding that a symbol can be given a meaning, be it temporary or permanent.

When children have acquired an understanding of the general principles of coding, it becomes one of the tools they use to learn; it is an integral part of learning specific new skills such as reading and mathematics. Some children develop the capacity for coding without specific teaching, whereas other children need to be taught how coding works. Mechanical coding is a method to develop this capacity, and it may be the stepping stone some children need to understand the underlying processes involved in reading; once this capacity is embedded, literacy skills can develop.

Links

Coding grows out of matching which is the understanding of how to make pairs. At the early stage, pairs are formed of two identical objects but at the later stages the concept expands and matching takes on the meaning of making pairs of items by their association. As an example, an orange and a banana can be a pair because they are both fruit. In coding, this concept of association is taken one step further as two symbols are paired arbitrarily and together they become a code.

Development of coding

From an early age, children learn to associate two events, one is linked to another and it acquires a set meaning; for example, dad puts the bib on the baby, and he understands this means food, or mum rattles her car keys, and this is recognised as the signal for going out in the car. These two examples illustrate how the child's understanding grows: by association one event come to represent another.

The big leap forward is when the child understands the idea of a temporary association between two symbols; this generally happens around the age of 60 months but some children develop this concept at an earlier age.

The teaching of mechanical coding, as the name implies, is a mechanical and rigid process; it follows a set format based on the processes of matching; the teaching stages are described in detail below alongside the supporting activities. Once the child has grasped the concept of coding, he usually applies this understanding spontaneously in everyday situations. It has now become one of his learning capacities.

Geoffrey Waldon also devised his own approach to reading which he called Functional Reading and the teaching of mechanical coding is part of this programme; however, it is outside the scope of this book to include the Functional Reading Programme.

Teaching mechanical coding

General set-up

Mechanical coding can be taught to a child who has reached the stage of mature matching. The child understands how to:

- ▶ Match without adult help.
- ▶ Use the H-board competently.
- ▶ Use a pointing finger to locate the next picture in a row.
- ▶ Scan around and persevere until the matching pairs have been found.

Coding is taught following the principles of the learning to learn lesson where every activity is taught through non-verbal, practical activities.

The instructions for mechanical coding are very detailed with lots of small steps to follow. Start by learning the process yourself and work through all the steps without the child. You will be able to move smoothly from one step in the activity to the next; the child will enjoy the challenge of working with the codes, it is an exciting activity to do together.

CODING ACTIVITIES

STAGE 1. EARLY CODING
Matching pictograms

The aim is to increase the awareness that a picture can be represented with a crude pictogram. The pictograms initially have a clear resemblance to the pictures, but they are changed gradually and become increasingly abstract, until eventually they look almost like symbols.

Matching pictures and pictograms

EQUIPMENT: H-board; set of matching cards, one half with line drawings and the second half simplified representations, known as pictograms.

ACTIVITY: Arrange the line drawings on the top row of the H-board.

Step 1. Give the child one pictogram at a time. Help him to find the match using the 'proofing' technique i.e. running the card along the length of the board and comparing it with all the pictures. Continue until all the drawings and pictograms have been matched up.

Step 2. Keep the pictures on the H-board but change a few of them around to create a new order; spread the pictograms on the table. With the child's hand, point to the first picture on the H-board, find the match and place the two together. Move on to the next picture in line and complete the board.

VARIATIONS: **a.** Use a second set of pictograms which is a simplification of the first; match this set to the original pictures.

b. Match the two sets of pictograms to each other.

SECTION 3: PRACTICAL ACTIVITIES

STAGE 2. ACTIVE CODING
Arbitrary associations

The aim is to teach the child that two random symbols can temporarily become a pair and belong together. The two symbols placed together become a code, and this will be the point of reference for making identical pairs of symbols.

Matching two different symbols in order

EQUIPMENT: Two H-boards, ❶ and ❷, two different sets of matching cards with arbitrary symbols, **A** and **B**.

ACTIVITY: **Step 1.** Separate set A. On H-board ❶, lay out half of the pairs on the top row and the matching half on H-board ❷. The cards should be in the same order on the two H-boards.

Step 2. Separate card set **B** and fill the bottom row on the first H-board with these cards. This makes a board with random pairs, such as ✱ is paired with ✖ and ◇ is paired with ⬤; this now represents a code to be referred to.

Step 3. Spread the remaining **B** cards on the table. Slowly and carefully guide the child to point to the first pairing on H-board ❶, and with the other hand point to the same symbol on ❷. Pick up and place the paired symbol card in the space below. In this way, H-board ❶ is copied, step by step, on ❷, with two rows of identically paired symbols.

SECTION 3: PRACTICAL ACTIVITIES

Matching by following a code

EQUIPMENT: Two H-boards, ❶ and ❷; two sets of matching cards with arbitrary symbols, **A** and **B,** used in the game above.

ACTIVITY: This activity is a development of 'Matching two different symbols in order' described above, but now the card order on the second H-board will be changed. Keep H-board ❶ the same as above with two rows of randomly paired symbols; this now represents a code and must be referred to in order to match up the cards on H-board ❷.

Step 1. On H-board ❷ change the order of set **A** and remove set **B;** this means the two H-boards will no longer be identical.

Step 2. Give the child one card from set **B,** locate this symbol on H-board ❶; point to this symbol, and then to its partner above.

Step 3. Find this same symbol on H-board ❷ and place the card in the empty space underneath; the two have been paired up according to the code. Repeat this with all the cards in set **B**.

VARIATION: Repeat steps 1 – 3, but this time move the two H-boards away from each other. Now the child has to look from one board to the other and he may even have to turn around or walk to another table to check the code on the H-board.

The code shows which two symbols are temporarily paired together. The child must be active in referencing the code, searching and checking to duplicate the match.

STAGE 3. MATURE CODING
Changing the code

This is the ability to follow arbitrary and changing codes. At this stage, pictures and symbols are used along with the objects they represent; words can also be incorporated into the coding games.

Follow the code

EQUIPMENT: Two H-boards, ❶ and ❷; two sets of matching cards with arbitrary symbols, **A** and **B**.

ACTIVITY: **Step 1.** Follow the steps outlined above for arbitrary matching; the child is required to refer to the code on H-board ❶ in order to match up the cards on board ❷.

Step 2. Change the order of cards **A** and **B** on H-board ❶, this means there is now a completely different pairing, it is a new code.

Step 3. Arrange the second half of set **A** on board ❷ as in the previous routines. Next spread the matching cards of set **B** on the table; point to the first in line on ❷, refer to the code on ❶; finally scan around and locate the matching card.

VARIATION: Change the materials used to create the new, arbitrary codes:

- ▶ Use unfamiliar shapes and symbols such as Chinese characters, or other unusual shapes.
- ▶ Words written in a foreign language; they have the appearance of patterns as opposed to being recognisable words.
- ▶ Objects can be randomly matched to various shapes.

The aim remains the same throughout – using a code to solve the problem, i.e. what does x mean in this context?

APPENDICES

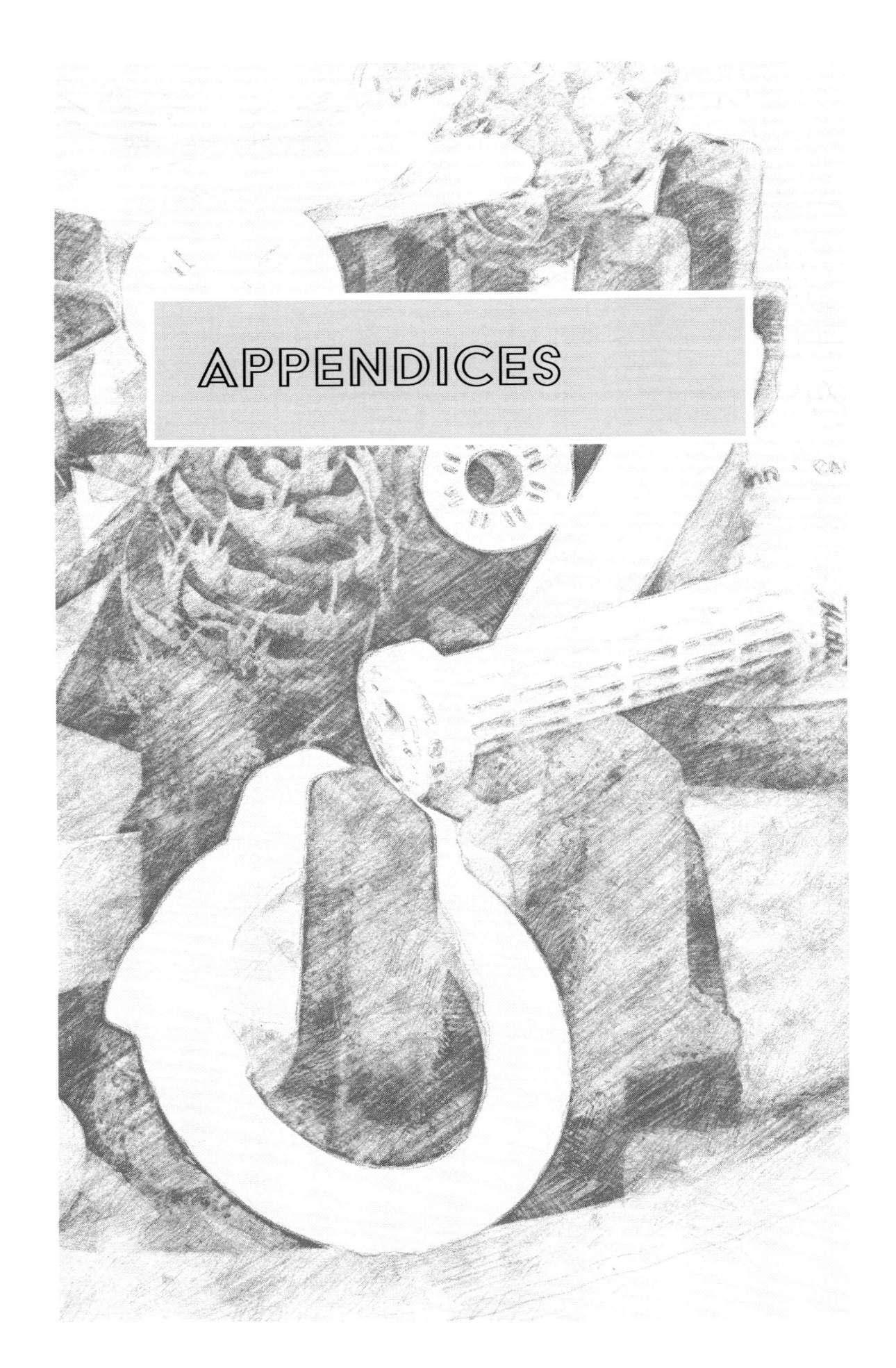

1: EQUIPMENT LIST

Basic learning to learn equipment

Start collecting: lots of the materials are everyday household items and 'loose bits'; other items can be made or purchased. It is not necessary to provide everything on the list, these are just suggestions; the key is to adapt and use the materials available in your setting. It is surprising how many games can be played with a small selection of such toys.

The list is organised according to the primary skill areas, this gives a quick overview of the range of useful materials. As mentioned previously, every piece of equipment can be incorporated into lots of different activities, working at all levels of development.

Always ensure the materials are safe to use.

Physical effort	*Materials*	
Placing into containers	**Containers:** bowls, buckets, tins, saucepans, empty boxes, plastic jugs, plastic flowerpots and saucers, baskets, yogurt pots	**Objects:** bricks, fir cones, beanbags, small bottles filled with sand and sealed, clothes pegs, jam jar lids, buttons
Range and use of space	Curtain rings or bangles Small plastic flowerpots Kitchen-roll holder Mug tree Boat with pegs	Pegboard Stick and hollow bricks Cardboard tube Stick, shorter than the child's arm Homemade posting boxes such as a coffee tin with a hole cut out in the lid
Complementary use of hands **Hand-held tools**	Wooden hammers or spoons Spoons and scoops Dustpan and brush Clothes pegs Short, solid wooden rod Large nuts and bolts	Tongs: BBQ, sugar or laundry Jars with screw-top lids Tins with different types of lids Bowl full of nuts or cones Tubs with lids and closing tabs
Continuant behaviour	Muffin tray Empty chocolate box Boat with pegs	Sets of small containers: flower pots, plastic cups, jars, plastic saucers etc. Sets of smaller objects: pegs, small bricks, reels, rings, lids, corks, keys etc.
Matching	Pairs of identical objects, 10 or more, which have little 'play interest' Pairs of non-identical objects e.g. two different bottle-tops, keys, cups, lids, rings, blocks, reels, yogurt pots etc. H-board	

Sorting	Sets of objects to sort, avoiding too much emphasis on colour. Collect: milk bottle tops, drink bottle tops, metal bottle tops, corks, stones, shells, washers, curtain rings, coins, buttons, mixed nuts etc. – anything! Commercial sorting sets like elephants, bears, people, dinosaurs etc. Shallow trays for sorting Sorting boards with 3x3 grids	
Seriation	Boxes in different sizes Stacking cups Pole with rings, decreasing in size	Set of identical blocks Objects in various lengths: toothpicks, pencils, straws, chopsticks
Drawing	Large pieces of paper Masking tape	Different types of crayons
Brick-building	Collection of objects in different forms, weight and size e.g. tins, small boxes, tubes, coasters, lids, straws Wooden building bricks e.g. Galt wooden play bricks	

Specialist Waldon equipment

These pieces of equipment are designed to be multifunctional and integrated. If the suggested measurements are employed the pegs from the boat will fit the pegboard and also inside the hollow bricks; the bricks fit into the spaces on the H-board and the sorting boards and so on. A skilled woodworker can make this equipment or it can be purchased from a few specialist makers; see Further Resources for contacts.

Boat

Two identical sides with 10 holes: 550 mm long. 60 mm wide, 40 mm high. 10 pegs to fit the holes: 52 mm tall and 27 mm diameter (a standard rod/ broom handle).

H-board

Each space 65 mm square, 10 spaces in two rows. The dividers are narrow battens, approx. 10 mm wide and 5 mm high.

Pegboard

This square board has rows of holes, 6x6 or larger. The holes and the pegs are identical to the pegs in the boat: 52 mm tall and 27 mm diameter.

Sorting boards

Boards with 3x3 grids; the spaces 65 mm square; the dividers are wooden battens approx. 10 mm wide, the same as the H-board.

Hollow bricks

The bricks are approx. 60 x 60 mm and 50 mm high and the hole is 30x30 mm; the pegs from the boat fit inside.

Stand

Round pole on a base; this is used for stacking the hollow bricks. The pole is tall enough to fit up to 10 bricks, approx. 600 mm high.

Blocks

Large collection, 20–30 pieces; approx. 55 mm square; the edges and corners can be sanded down for a smoother feel.

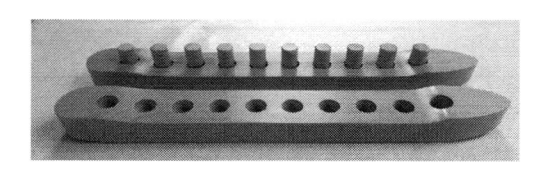

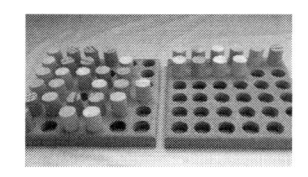

Learning to learn: *Lesson plan and feedback form*

Name:	Date:

Track: 0 = level not yet reached   / = emerging skill   X = competent skill

APPROACH TO TASK	Track	Observations
Is able to become and stay engaged		
Can continue activity unsupported		
Accepts change/variations in the activity		
Any signs of anxiety?		
Challenging behaviours impeding learning?		
General comments		

LEVEL 1: FUNDAMENTAL MOVEMENT ABILITIES

Content	Abilities	Track	Activities	Observations/recommendations
1. The appearance of physical effort	Reaches out			
	Grasps spontaneously			
	Will let go of objects			
	Places objects into tubs etc.			
	Is effortful			
	Continues unsupported			
2. Range and use of space	Crosses midline L/R/both			
	Reaches up/out/down/behind			
	Locates objects out of sight			
3. Picking up and putting in	Repeats action of picking up and putting in			
	Places an object in a defined space e.g. on a grid			
	Chooses between objects			
	Returns to the source of the objects			
4. Complementary use of hands and tool-use	Holds tools firmly in the hand			
	Bangs/scrapes rhythmically			
	Uses a scoop/spoon			
	Uses hands together, one as support to complete the task			
	Two-handed, twist lids on/off			
	Adapts the use of a tool to solve a problem			

LEVEL 2: CONTINUANT CAPACITY

Abilities	Track	Activities	Observations/recommendations
Makes a line of objects and moves them one by one to create a new line			
Can continue a 'double line', one element with another on top, repeated in a line			
Two-step sequence: remove the element on top & replace it with a different object, all along the line			
Continues a sequence of moving three sorts of objects in a set order			

LEVEL 3: LEARNING TO LEARN CAPACITIES

Content	Activities *Record stage: Early, Active, Mature*	Observations/recommendations
Matching		
Sorting		
Seriation		
Drawing		
Brick-building		
Coding		

3: LEARNING TO LEARN CAPACITIES

Developmental framework

Developmental stages with significant markers

MATCHING		
Stage	**Abilities**	✓
Stage 1: Early matching Making pairs of two identical objects	Understands the game of making pairs by placing two identical objects together	
	Can look for an object to match the one he has been shown	
	Can ignore other objects in the process of selecting the match	
Stage 2: Active matching Matching the model by actively seeking and making comparisons	Can play the matching game independently, scanning and comparing two objects to make the decision	
	Can make pairs of non-identical objects such as two different cups, stones, clothes pegs, keys etc.	
	Understands how to play on the H-board	
	Can match pictures which are very different	
	Can match simple shapes, all monochrome	

	Can match shapes and ignore redundant information, for example:
	    Set of shapes where the colour is irrelevant
	    Shapes with variation in the backgrounds like dots, lines or squiggles
	    Different shapes in two sizes	

Stage 3: Mature matching The best fit selecting by looking and making mental comparisons	Can look around to find two that make a pair, not identical but a good enough fit	
	Can consider two separate elements such as colour and shape	
	Can match two shapes side by side in different colours	
	Can distinguish between overlapping shapes	
	Can attend to the orientation of shapes and figures	
	Can examine pictures for fine details and variations	
	Can ignore irrelevant information	

	Can match pictures by association, such as:
	    Knife and fork, coat and hat, rabbit and hutch
	    Two tools, two toys, two modes of transports, two living things etc.	

Comments		

SORTING		
Stage	**Abilities**	✓
Stage 1: Early sorting Separating identical objects into sets	Can separate into sets which are distinctly different such as a) bricks, b) pencils and c) hazelnuts	
	Can sort objects that are very similar but not identical such as a) corks, b) keys and c) mixed nuts, comparing every new item with the sets in the trays	
	Can sort sets of cards with identical pictures or patterns using the sorting boards	
Stage 2: Active sorting Creating sets by sorting collections of objects or picture cards	Can sort into three to five sets, objects which are not identical but clearly belong together in groups, responding to the seeded trays	
	Can sort into three to five sets, picture cards which are not identical but clearly belong together in groups, responding to the seeded boards	
	Can sort a collection with three sets of non-identical objects, making decisions about objects which could fall into one of two categories	
	Can sort a collection with three sets mixed together, starting with two seeded trays, then spontaneously creates a third category in a non-seeded tray	

	Can sort cards with graphic patterns with variations:
	    Shapes in varying sizes
	    Irrelevant details like background pattern
	    Variations in the shapes themselves	

	Can sort cards with pictures with variations:
	    Irrelevant details like background pattern
	    Variations in the pictures themselves
	    Attending to fragments of the whole such as parts of a shop/car/playground	

Stage 3: Mature sorting Classifying according to a variety of attributes	Can focus on specific features to define a category and make decisions where the items belong. For example, broad categories such as a) wood, b) cylinder c) metal, a metal tube fits into b & c, a wooden cylinder fits a & b.	
	Can make the decision about sorting criteria, then adjust or change to create new categories. For example, a) red bricks, b) pencils and c) various animals, may be changed to a) everything red, b) pencils and c) small animals and d) big animals	
	Can classify according to abstract and knowledge-based categories, e.g. a) lives in the sea, b) on the ground, c) in the trees; another example, the object will a) sink or b) float; the object will a) bounce, b) roll or c) fall flat; spiders can be: a) poisonous or b) harmless etc.	
	Intersectional sorting: Can sort two overlapping sets using a grid matrix, the criteria are observable features such as shape, pattern, orientation	
	Intersectional sorting: Can work out the criteria and sort into overlapping sets accordingly	
Comments		

SERIATION

Stage	Abilities	✓
Stage 1: Early seriation		
Chaining objects in long rows	Can move lines of objects, one by one, from one place to another	
	Can continue a solid line of objects working in different directions, from left to right, right to left, diagonally across, away from or towards the body	
	Can continue a line of objects with small gaps between them; the objects are no longer touching each other	
Stage 2: Active seriation		
a. Alternating sequence of objects	Can distribute one object into each container, all lined up in a row	
	Can continue a sequence of alternating objects after initial support, for example: i) red block, blue block, red, blue… ii) cork, walnut, cork, walnut… etc. iii) tall cylinder, short cylinder, tall cylinder, short etc.	
b. Getting bigger or smaller in size using 3-D objects	b. Getting bigger or smaller: Shows awareness of the different sizes of blocks when building a tower three to four blocks high	
	b. Getting bigger or smaller: Can fit together a small set of nesting cups, with some trial and error in doing so	
Stage 3: Mature seriation		
a. Creating repeating patterns with objects or pictures	Can continue a repeating pattern from independent observation	
	Can continue a repeating pattern with three, four or more than four elements	
	Generates own pattern sequences	
b. Organising into size order, building up and along	Can organise 3-dimensional objects (e.g. blocks, square rods) according to size by building up	
	Can organise objects such as a set of cylinders or triangles in the horizontal plane, getting smaller/getting bigger	
	Can arrange flat shapes according to size in one long line	
	Can fill in the gap in a series by extrapolating from the pattern, e.g. understands the order of birthday cakes from the increasing number of candles	
Comments		

DRAWING

Stage	Abilities	✓
Stage 1: Early drawing Making a mark with a tool	Can hold a tool in the hand and tap or scrape with it	
	Pays attention to the marks made, such as with a crayon on paper or lines in the sand	
Stage 2: Active drawing Drawing lines in different directions and patterns	Can draw lines with large movements in front of the body	
	Can scribble with large, circular movements, moving in different directions	
	Can stop and start a line	
	Can draw a continuous line	
	Is interested in watching another person draw (but does not copy yet)	
Stage 3: Mature drawing Drawing shapes and pictures and observing in order to copy	Can draw lines in different directions	
	Can join up two lines	
	Can draw simple shapes and might spontaneously name the picture such as sun or car	
	Attempts to reproduce complex figures like a cross within a circle; gives attention to the elements but it may not resemble the original	
	Can draw simple pictures, attending to the different elements and how they are positioned and oriented in relation to each other, like the wheels on a car	
Comments		

BRICK-BUILDING		
Stage	Abilities	✓
Stage 1: Early brick-building Piling with lots of different materials	Can place objects randomly on a pile	
	Can tolerate the objects moving or falling off the pile	
	Can place objects deliberately with the intention to make them balance and stay in a certain place	
Stage 2: Active brick-building Planning to build and doing so with purpose; the model might not resemble the stated plan	Can place bricks deliberately: on top, alongside or behind each other	
	Can decide on a model to make and starts to build with that in mind; there may be a change of plan during the process of building and the model becomes something else	
	Can copy simple relationships between elements by watching the adult place one brick behind another, one in front of another or creating a bridge between two blocks	
Stage 3: Mature brick-building Copying and building by analysing a model as well as designing his own structures	Can copy a symmetrical model with up to six bricks, by looking at the finished model	
	Can copy a model with several elements	
	Can copy a model with hidden elements or sub-structures	
	Can create a model by following a step by step instruction or by interpreting a diagram	
Comments		

CODING		
Stage	Abilities	✓
Stage 1: Early coding: Matching pictograms	Can match a photograph and a drawing of the same object	
	Can match a drawing to a crude outline (pictogram) of the same object	
Stage 2: Active coding: Arbitrary associations	Can follow a code to make pairs of pictures accordingly, i.e. two random pictures or shapes are placed together as a pair; this is replicated to make identical pairs	
Stage 3: Mature coding: Changing the code	Can refer to a code to establish the link between two objects/ pictures/ shapes	
	Understands a code can change, for example in one exercise ■ = ★, this is later changed and now ■ = 🐘 and ★ = 🐈	
Comments		

4: EXTRACTS FROM LESSON FEEDBACK

The following extracts show examples of observations made during the working sessions with a child. They are used to reflect on the abilities the child demonstrated in the session and will help to decide on the content of the next session. The detailed descriptions of all levels and appropriate activities can be found in chapters 7, 8 and 9 and the Developmental Framework in Appendix 3.

APPROACH TO TASK

Extract: Helen

Is able to become and stay engaged:

Helen very quickly engaged and she has the ability to remain so for quite some time. She was curious throughout the session. Her enjoyment was clearly evident.

Can continue unsupported:

Helen can continue on her own. At times, she needed to slow down to let the adult guide her through a new activity. She showed great perseverance and desire to solve problems on her own.

Acceptance of change and variations:

Helen has a preference for the familiar and sometimes wanted to continue in her own way. She can accept subtle changes if these are introduced gradually.

Any signs of anxiety:

She displayed signs of unease when new activities were presented. Helen got distracted and distressed by high-pitched noises in the background: these clearly caused her some discomfort.

Challenging behaviours impeding learning:

None displayed in this session.

General comments:

Helen was not used to being guided hand over hand; she appeared to be touch sensitive. With some activities she was able to attend to an adult demonstrating slowly and pointing; this approach can work for some activities but not all. She was very comfortable working in the non-verbal environment. Helen needed time to process the information, not to be rushed, when she had to carry out a sequence of actions.

LEVEL 1: FUNDAMENTAL MOVEMENT ABILITIES

Extract: Neil

Observations and recommendations

Neil can reach out and pick up an object without support. He sometimes forgot where the containers were placed, and would lose the momentum of posting. Neil lacked the ability to carry on with a steady rhythm, he slowed down and stalled. This will affect his ability to continue a movement sequence. He will benefit from strong, rhythmic activities of picking up and putting in, as well as the earlier stage of 'banging and scraping'.

Neil's core stability appeared quite weak, for example, he wobbled a bit when he reached out and he often leaned on one arm whilst using the other. Though he can pick up and place objects, his grasp is weak and it needs both strengthening and work on dexterity. Neil understood the tasks of using two hands together such as holding a large scoop and sweeping a brick into it but his underlying coordination difficulties impacted on his ability to complete the steps.

This area of development is important for his continued progress and time must be spent on developing his fundamental movement abilities; incorporate a large variety of tool-use exercises and consider a wide range of movements.

LEVEL 2: CONTINUANT CAPACITY

Extract: Ayaan

Observations and recommendations

Ayaan can create single and double lines with bricks and other small pieces; he is most comfortable working in the space in front of him. He needs to explore a wider area: move the lines, piece by piece, from one table to another, change the direction and work from left to right and then in reverse. He understands and can make a sequence by placing one object on top of another to complete a row. Ayaan's ability to exchange the piece on top with a different object in a set order, is developing; this is evidence of the emerging continuant capacity. Continue with a variety of activities at this early level, moving two different sets of objects from one place to another in an organised and planned fashion as well as swapping one piece for another along a row.

LEVEL 3

Matching – Early: Making pairs of two identical objects

Extract: Georgie
Observations and recommendations

The early stages of learning the pairing game requires the facilitator to guide the child's hands; Georgie was reluctant to accept this help and it triggered some challenging behaviour: swiping the table and throwing the pieces. Georgie was kept focused by continuing slowly and steadily, and reducing the physical support as soon as possible. Georgie quickly learnt the rules of the pairing game and it was clear that he enjoyed it. He managed to scan the six pairs spread over the double table. I introduced rogue pieces to increase the size of the pool; this compelled Georgie to look more closely and make many more comparisons, 'Is it this one?' This increased the challenge for him. Continue to develop the pairing game with variations whilst staying within his comfort zone: play with different pairs, use a large area to search for the match and gradually increase the number of pairs or number of rogue pieces.

LEVEL 3

Seriation – Active: Alternating sequences of objects

Extract: Anita
Observations and recommendations

Anita started by making single chains of objects, then adding a second line in front. She was continuant and independent in doing so. She was able to separate the two chains into containers, alternating between the two sets of objects. I changed the objects and started to build an alternating sequence, then guided Anita's hands through the steps. She quickly carried on and continued on her own. She demonstrated the ability to continue alternating sequences with several different sets of objects.

A third element was introduced: a block with a button on top, then a jam-jar lid - repeated. She was able to attend to two of the elements, sometimes she left the button out, sometimes the jam-jar lid. She is on the cusp of being able to create sequences with three elements in an ordered sequence. Continue with lots of different alternating sequences whilst also including the joint elements e.g. a cup with a spatula, into these sequences. This 2+1 approach makes a bridge to the next stage: sequences with three elements.

LEVEL 3

Brick-building – Mature: Analysing a model and copying it

Extract: Olivia

Observations and recommendations

We started by playing the pairing game with the Galt bricks, leaving us with two identical sets of bricks. Olivia watched as I slowly built a model with several different bricks, including a bridging piece; she copied this model quickly. The next model had a supporting element that wasn't visible on the finished model; she spent a lot of time comparing her own effort to my model, trying to work out why two pieces wouldn't stay in place. She experimented and arrived at a solution she was happy with. Olivia also made a model for me to copy; she enjoyed the opportunity to create her own structures. Continue to experiment with three-dimensional structures: alter, add and remove pieces. Olivia is also ready to start looking at diagrams and recreate the given models.

GENERAL COMMENTS

Extract: Carl

Carl enjoyed the non-verbal lesson and he showed great determination and perseverance. He has some weaknesses in his fundamental movement abilities, bodily integration and hand skills. He is developing continuant capacity and he is approaching early stages of the learning to learn capacities.

Continue to incorporate regular sessions into Carl's weekly programme and balance these lessons along the lines of:

60% on fundamental movement abilities

30% continuant capacity

10% on the learning to learn capacities

This will give Carl the opportunity to explore widely at his level and from these experiences his general understanding will grow.

5: FREQUENTLY ASKED QUESTIONS

I want to say 'Good boy'; why shouldn't I praise him?

The structured session simulates the time when a child is playing on his own. He is exploring and investigating and he doesn't know what he is going to discover, because he doesn't know yet! He learns from the unexpected discoveries and his understanding grows from there. For the child, the motivation comes from within and the pleasure comes from the effort and the doing. Praise is an adult response; it does not promote the child's understanding in this learning context.

See 'Understanding Understanding' in chapter 2, and a fuller discussion about praise in chapter 5.

I think the child is bored, it's all too easy for him.

Learning to learn is a developmental programme and as we can continue to learn throughout life, there is no upper limit. That means, if the child is not fully engaged, the facilitator hasn't got the levels quite right; there are always exciting ways to develop the child's thinking skills. The learning foundations are movement-based and a solid physical warm-up through effortful activities helps to focus and to get the energy flowing. There is a short video of Geoffrey Waldon talking about 'boredom' in the Library Index on the Waldon Association website, listed as *This is boring ... 'boredom' ... lack of understanding*; here he explains why the activities are both meaningful and enjoyable for the child and never boring!

Why is it important to keep going? Maybe the child has had enough.

When young children play on their own, they will naturally be playing at their current developmental level. They start with activities they know well, then variations begin to occur and new games develop; for this to happen, they need time to become fully immersed, and this is why it is recommended to continue the activities for longer than is normally expected. The skilled facilitator can create learning experiences which move up and down the developmental levels, and the child is constantly experiencing success. There is obviously a point where the session must be concluded, and the sensitive adult knows when that point has been reached. In chapter 5 there is a discussion about ways of keeping the child engaged.

What do I do if the child makes a mistake?

It will depend on the situation, but usually a 'mistake' reflects the child's level of understanding and maybe the task is too difficult. The general advice is: try to figure out why he made the decision he did, then adjust the activity so he can succeed. Don't draw attention to the 'mistake', but instead help him to learn. Take, for example, a matching game: the child picks up the incorrect match; simply put it down again and show him the right one. If he has paired two cards wrongly, remove one card and present it again later and point to the correct match; it is not a test but always a learning opportunity.

Why is it important to stop in the middle of an activity?

When young children play and explore, they do not have a plan with an end goal. Their play is open-ended and they do not seek to finish. Restarting or changing an activity mid-flow during the session, emulates the natural rhythm of self-directed play. It has the added benefit of encouraging flexibility and tolerance, and it helps to prevent the fixation on closure which some children have.

What do I do if the child picks up two bricks instead of one?

This is a very common behaviour and there can be several different reasons for it:

- ▶ He doesn't understand how to pick up just one at a time.
- ▶ It is a labour-saving behaviour arising from underlying movement challenges.
- ▶ Some children do it as a bit of a tease: what are you going to do about it?

If a child has picked up two bricks, it might be possible to push the extra brick out of his hand with a finger and post the remaining one; this communicates 'one at a time' as intended. But don't make the behaviour into an issue: it is preferable to prevent it and practise the correct way of picking up. This can be encouraged by either spreading the bricks over a wider area, giving the child one at a time or by using larger bricks so only one fits in the hand! There are recommendations for dealing with these challenges in chapter 5.

What do I do if the child throws the stuff around?

Pay no attention and continue with the activity though this is easier said than done! Do not reprimand the child or make him pick it up again, the game should continue regardless. Try to have extra material within reach to avoid getting up if all has gone flying. It is a challenging behaviour the child has to unlearn and feeling successful is one way of achieving that. It may be advisable to change the difficulty of the task because the behaviour can be caused by the child feeling too challenged. Tidy up at the end of the session, after the child has gone.

What do I do if the child goes rigid and refuses to pick up the pieces?

This behaviour can be perceived as challenging; however, all behaviour has a reason. When the child goes rigid it is akin to a freeze response which can be due to feelings of anxiety or uncertainty about the task; it can also be a learnt behaviour that has worked well for the child in the past, 'what are you going to do about it?'

I find the best way to re-engage the child is to continue on my own, I don't pay attention to the behaviour, I simply carry on as if he is taking part. As a rule, the child soon relaxes, starts to pay attention and he gets involved again.

Read more about challenging behaviours in chapters 4 and 5.

6: FURTHER INFORMATION

Further reading

My primary resources are Dr Geoffrey Waldon's own writing and these are available on the Waldon Association website, **www.waldonassociation.org.uk** There can be found a large number of papers by Waldon explaining his insights and approach including the paper, *'Why such emphasis on 'picking-up and putting-in' and on 'banging and scraping?'* which I referred to in the text. There is also an outline for a proposed book which he never completed as well as transcripts of interviews between Waldon and some early practitioners in the field.

Richard Brooks worked very closely with Geoffrey Waldon and he has a deep understanding of his ideas. On the above-mentioned website there is a transcript of his interview with Waldon: *Reinforcement, Autism and the 'Remote' Child*. He has also written a paper, analysing and describing in detail an assessment session carried out by Waldon: *Maria: Description of an Asocial Lesson*, which is in the Library Index. This paper gives a great insight into the girl's cognitive levels of functioning, highlights her emotional fragility and how attuned the adult must be to those needs.

The Early Years Foundation Stage (EYFS) covers the age from birth to five years old; the EYFS (2017) described development in terms of three primary areas: communication and language, physical development and personal, social and emotional development; in addition are the four specific areas: literacy, mathematics, understanding the world and expressive arts and design. The present book covers the developmental stages in the EYFS, but has as the main focus the development of early cognitive skills; in the EYFS this is presented as an overlap between physical development, literacy, numeracy and understanding of the world.

The EYFS states that 'each area of learning and development must be implemented through planned, purposeful play and through a mix of adult-led and child-initiated activity' and 'children learn by leading their own play, and by taking part in play which is guided by adults. There is an ongoing judgement to be made by practitioners about the balance between them' (EYFS 1.8, 2017). The Learning to learn approach is the tool which teachers need to support children who require more active guidance to acquire the fundamental skills for learning, thus equipping these children with the abilities to learn through their own play.

The EYFS guidance can be found at:

Department of Education, *Statutory framework for the early year's foundation stage. Setting the Standards for learning, development and care for children from birth to five.*
Published: 3 March 2017. Effective: 3 April 2017

Books and websites

www.waldonassociation.org.uk
Papers written by Dr Geoffrey Waldon and early practitioners in the field.

www.autismandunderstanding.com
This website belongs to Walter Solomon where he provides a rare opportunity to watch videos of Geoffrey Waldon working with children; the videos are short snippets from longer sessions, accompanied by written explanations of the purposes of the activities. The videos are a product of their time, and my own insights into conducting a session have changed in the intervening years. There is also footage of Walter Solomon working with children in a special school, using his interpretation of the approach. Several of his videos last 30 minutes or more and they are great examples of how children can enjoy activities and concentrate for long periods of time.

Autism and Understanding: The Waldon Approach to Child Development
Walter Solomon with Chris Holland and Mary Jo Middleton, Sage Publication, London (2012).
This tells the inspirational story of Solomon's son and the success of using the Waldon Approach with him.

Every Child Can Learn
Katrin Stroh, Thelma Robinson and Alan Proctor, Sage Publication, London (2008).
This is a programme which incorporates some of Geoffrey Waldon's ideas; it is aimed at parents and professionals working with children with developmental delay.

www.autismseendevelopmentally.org
Sibylle Janert uses the approach with families in the home; she has found that it complements the relationship-based DIRFloortime® intervention she also uses.

Practical resources

www.toyswithtools.com
A source for wooden toys as designed by Geoffrey Waldon. They are made to order by David Palmer, who can be contacted via the website.

www.autismandunderstanding.com
Wooden developmental toys and books are available via Walter Solomon's website.

Contact

Please contact me on **hawkinsmerete@gmail.com**
I deliver an extensive training programme to special schools, introducing the ***Learning to learn*** approach, which I complement by working alongside the staff to demonstrate the approach with children in the classroom.

I work with parents, advising them on the benefits of the approach and how to use the techniques with their child at home.

Printed in Great Britain
by Amazon